CONTENTS

D-DAY
AND THE INVASION OF NORMANDY

Anthony Kemp

DISCOVERIES

HARRY N. ABRAMS, INC., PUBLISHERS

In June 1944 World War II was already nearly five years old. Adolf Hitler's invasion of Poland in September 1939 had been followed by a string of Nazi victories that culminated in an assault on Belgium in May 1940. British and French troops rushed to the aid of their ally, but were slowly beaten back toward the French town of Dunkirk, on the English Channel. Under constant fire, the Allies miraculously succeeded in evacuating over 300,000 soldiers from Dunkirk's beaches. Four years later, some of these men would return to take part in D-Day, the greatest amphibious operation ever undertaken.

CHAPTER I
THE ORIGINS OF OVERLORD

In 1940 Britain's Prime Minister Winston Churchill (opposite) vowed to continue the struggle against Nazi Germany. All along the coastline of German-occupied France, the Germans waited for the day when the Allies would strike back. A detail of Hitler's "Atlantic Wall" is at right.

Between these two events, the Germans had been chased out of North Africa and were in retreat in Russia. In Italy, following the collapse of Benito Mussolini's Fascist regime, Allied armies were beginning to break through the German defensive line. But Hitler's stranglehold on Europe had yet to be broken.

In 1940, at a time of seeming defeat, the recently installed prime minister of Great Britain, Winston Churchill, reluctantly agreed that the only way to stop the Germans was to bring their forces to battle in France. And to do that, three things were necessary: First, the immediate threat of a Nazi invasion of Britain had to be removed; second, a new British army had to be trained and equipped; and third and most important of all, American manpower and industrial might would have to be harnessed to the task.

At the Time, There Were No Specialized Ships for Landing Troops and the British Forces Had No Experience with Amphibious Landings

Churchill, however, was desperate to come to grips with the enemy—if only in a limited way—and, to that end, he established an organization called Combined Operations to coordinate raids on the continent and test methods of invasion.

Such exercises may have boosted morale in Britain at a time when that country felt alone in its opposition to the might of the Nazi war machine, but they had little real effect. The tide began to turn, however, when Hitler—after overrunning Greece and Yugoslavia—ill-advisedly invaded Russia in June of 1941. The German armies swept forward to the gates of Moscow, but there they were brought to a standstill by the

deliberate and effective retreat of the Soviet army and the onset of the brutal Russian winter. Hitler's fate was sealed on 7 December 1941, when his Japanese allies mounted a surprise attack on the US naval station in Pearl Harbor, Hawaii, and America entered the war.

Allied Strategy in Early 1942 Called for Primary Emphasis to be Placed on the Defeat of Germany

At a conference in Washington, D.C., in January, the British and American sides met to coordinate policy. There the responsibility for commanding the Allied war effort was given to the newly formed Combined Chiefs of Staff, accountable to both the president of the United States and the prime minister of

In September 1942 the German Sixth Army reached the city of Stalingrad (now Volgograd, left). Street by street, the Russian forces resisted, and two months later they mounted a victorious counterattack. This marked the turning point of the war in the east and the start of the gradual German retreat from Russia.

The first major raid carried out by British Commandos was against the Norwegian-owned Lofoten Islands in March 1941 (below). Only a thousand men took part, but the landing was unopposed, and all returned safely. Nine thousand tons of enemy shipping were destroyed. As a result of this and other raids in the area, Hitler stationed 300,000 troops in Norway instead of France.

Great Britain. Within this body, strong differences of opinion soon surfaced. Churchill and his chiefs of staff favored attacking Germany through the Mediterranean, the "underbelly" of Europe, beginning with an invasion of German-occupied French colonies in North Africa. The Americans, however, led by US Army chief of staff General George C. Marshall, were fearful of a total Russian collapse and argued for an all-out assault across the English Channel in hopes of drawing maximum

Lord Louis Mountbatten (below), a cousin of King George VI and an officer in the Royal Navy, was made director of Combined Operations and helped lay plans for the forthcoming invasion of Europe.

LE REVEIL DU NORD

UNE ACTION DESESPÉRÉE SUR L'ORDRE DE MOSCOU

DANS LES ENVIRONS DE DIEPPE,

une grande tentative de débarquement anglo-américaine est brisée en 10 heures

German forces away from the Red Army. The conference ended with the Allies agreeing in principle to a landing on the coast of France in 1942 if necessary to divert German attention from Russia (a plan they named Sledgehammer) and a large-scale invasion of France in early 1943 (a proposal they named Roundup). Conflicts in strategy between the two Western allies cast a shadow over the next several months of planning for the defeat of Germany. While in agreement about the need to help the hard-pressed Russians, American and British strategists had a harder time agreeing on whether they should mount an all-out attack or merely a diversionary maneuver. Given the lack of landing craft and the

The human and material costs of the Dieppe raid were enormous, in spite of the valuable lessons learned. The losses were also a terrible blow to Allied morale at a time when the Germans still seemed unbeatable. Its failure led the Allied staffs to rethink their invasion plans.

fact that German submarines, or U-boats, were still masters of the Atlantic, such plans were at this stage somewhat academic. For without adequate shipping, a massive movement of men and military equipment from America could never be accomplished.

It was deemed imperative, however, to bring American troops into action, and thus it was proposed that the Allies should first concentrate on running the Germans out of North Africa—a plan labeled Operation Torch.

The Lessons of the Dieppe Raid

An important event that greatly influenced the planning of future landings in Normandy was the gallant but suicidal raid conducted by Canadian forces on the small French port of Dieppe in August 1942. The operation was a virtual disaster for the Allies, but did highlight for them the deficiencies in their plans for a major cross-Channel assault.

The aim of the

The Dieppe raid was the first time that an attempt was made to land tanks to support an infantry assault. The type used was the British-designed Churchill Mark III (below), which weighed a hefty forty tons. Later, modified versions of the Churchill tank landed on D-Day.

raid had been to put a sizeable force ashore and to hold the port for a short period before re-embarking, thereby testing the feasibility of a larger-scale invasion of France. It was also hoped that the raid would persuade the Germans to divert troops and aircraft from along the Russian front.

An infantry division supported by heavy tanks and Commando forces was landed on the beach, but— as there had been no preliminary bombardment of the German defenses from the sea—the Canadians were immediately pinned down by the German artillery contained in bunkers along the shore. Despite hundreds of acts of individual gallantry, over three thousand men (about half the total force) were killed, wounded, or captured. Nazi news reports boasted that Hitler's forces had decisively defeated a major invasion attempt.

But the lessons of Dieppe, learned at so great a cost, were many. Several of the smaller types of landing craft had been fabricated of plywood and were easily shot to pieces during the approach. As well, communications between the headquarters ship and the units on shore were catastrophically inept, and the force commander had little idea of what was happening on the front line. It also became abundantly clear to the planners that a huge force would be needed at the point of attack and that specialized equipment would be needed to move troops and equipment off the beaches quickly and safely. After the war, Lord Louis Mountbatten, director of Combined Operations, is said to have commented that for every

Dwight D. Eisenhower was raised in Kansas, one of seven sons of a poor family. Graduated from West Point in 1915, he then spent most of his army career before World War II in staff appointments. In 1942 he was given command of American forces in Britain and named commander of the Allied landings in North Africa (pictured below). During Overlord, Eisenhower was criticized for not taking firmer control, yet this calm, unassuming man commanded fierce loyalty and is widely credited with holding the Allied armies together with his charm and diplomacy.

soldier who died at Dieppe, ten were saved on D-Day. ("D-Day" is the military term designating the date set for launching any operation, but in modern history it is usually assumed to refer to the events of 6 June 1944).

Dieppe obviated any further discussion of Sledgehammer for 1942, and the planners concentrated their efforts on a North African invasion—although Operation Roundup, the full invasion of France planned for 1943, was still very much on the table.

Operation Torch

The supreme commander selected by the Allied leaders for the African campaign was, at the time, a relatively unknown American brigadier general named Dwight D. Eisenhower, a capable staff officer whose highest troop command to date had been that of a battalion. Hastily promoted to general, "Ike," as he was affectionately known, formed an Allied staff, which included an American deputy commander, General

Field Marshal Erwin Rommel (below) served with distinction in World War I. In late 1943 Hitler appointed him to command Army Group B and gave him responsibility for the defense of Normandy. In 1944 Rommel committed suicide rather than face trial for his alleged involvement in a plot to assassinate the Führer.

Mark Clark, and three British deputies for air, sea, and ground operations. The logistical problems were immense. Troops and supplies all had to be brought to the area across open ocean, subject to constant threat from German U-boats and land-based bombers. The American forces had been hastily assembled, and many of the units could be only partially familiarized with their new mission.

Despite these and other difficulties, Operation Torch was an unqualified success. And when General Bernard L. Montgomery and the British Eighth Army—having trounced German Field Marshal Erwin Rommel and his Afrika Korps at El-Alamein in October 1942—joined Torch forces in Tunisia in May 1943, the remaining German troops were forced to surrender. The Allies now had a stable springboard for launching operations against German-held areas in the Mediterranean, and Eisenhower gained the well-deserved respect of the Allied planners.

COSSAC: "Architects of D-Day"

In January 1943 President Roosevelt, Prime Minister Churchill, and the Combined Chiefs of Staff met in Casablanca, a seaport on Morocco's west coast. At this meeting it was decided to postpone Roundup until 1944 and to establish an Anglo-American headquarters in London to explore all site possibilities for a landing in France. This staff was to be headed by Lieutenant General Frederick E. Morgan of the British Army; American Brigadier General Ray W. Barker was named as his deputy. As Morgan's new title was Chief of Staff to the Supreme Allied Commander (a figure who had not yet been appointed), his team soon became known by the acronym COSSAC.

COSSAC's assigned task was to plan Overlord (this code name

The conference held at Casablanca in January 1943 was an opportunity for the two main Western leaders, Winston Churchill and Franklin Delano Roosevelt, to settle their differences in the company of their joint chiefs of staff. The Allies also had to contend with rivalries between the French factions. Watched by the two leaders, Generals Charles de Gaulle and Henri Giraud exchange a brief handshake (below).

replaced the earlier Roundup), a full-scale invasion of Europe, to take place as early as possible in 1944. From the outset, the planners were faced by a serious lack of naval equipment, as German submarines in the Atlantic in the early months of 1943 were still sinking more tonnage than could be replaced by the shipyards. By that summer, however, the

Battle of the Atlantic (German U-boat attacks on British ships) appeared to have been won—thanks largely to the protective escorts of American warships and advances in warfare technology.

Where to Land?

A series of factors had to be taken into consideration as COSSAC determined where the actual invasion would take place. The shortest route would be the logical choice, as it would mean less time at sea, faster resupply, and easier air support from airfields in England. In practical terms, that pointed to the Pas-de-Calais region of northern France. The Germans, however, realizing this, had concentrated their heaviest defenses there.

Another drawback of the Pas-de-Calais region was that there were no large harbors on a par with those of Le Havre (to the north of the Seine River) and Cherbourg (on Cotentin Peninsula). After weighing several other possibilities, the Allied planners eventually decided upon the relatively unfortified beaches of Normandy, some 150 miles southwest of Pas-de-Calais.

The American genius for improvisation was put to good use building the "Liberty" ships that would ferry men and supplies across the Atlantic (above). In special shipyards that operated day and night, traditional time-consuming methods of construction were abandoned in favor of welding the ships together in large sections—the same technique that is used in the automobile industry.

The planners soon realized that this area was indeed ideal, as it was separated by the Seine from the areas of France that had been most strenuously armed by Hitler. They believed that if the bridges across the Seine could be destroyed, Hitler's response would be slowed and the Allies might be given sufficient time to stockpile men and equipment in Normandy for the grand push across northern France into Germany.

After much research, the COSSAC team decided on four specific beaches—code-named Omaha, Gold, Juno, and Sword—on the northern coast of Cotentin Peninsula near the mouths of the Orne and Vire rivers. General Morgan and his planners devised a scheme that entailed landing three divisions (about thirty thousand men, with twenty thousand more in reserve) on the beaches and dropping two airborne divisions (one US and one British, using both paratroopers and gliders) nearby. This plan was unanimously approved at a conference held in Quebec in August 1943.

The Opposition

Following the invasion of France in the summer of 1940, the German Army had remained in occupation of the country's entire coastline. The territory allocated to the Vichy regime—the pro-German government of France—was confined to the interior. Originally the French coast was seen as a springboard for a German invasion

The Pas-de-Calais region was the obvious place for the Allies to land. This part of France was closest to the industrial centers of Germany, and the attackers could be easily supported by fighter aircraft based in England, just over twenty miles away. In 1940 the Germans had used the same reasoning as they plotted their intended invasion the other direction.

LONDON

Dover

Southampton Portsmouth Newhaven   Calais
              Shoreham   Hastings   Boulogne

Portland-   Touquet
Weymouth   Isle of Wight

                                    Dieppe   GERMAN
                                              FIFTEENTH
Cherbourg   Fécamp   ARMY
                    Arromanches Le Havre
                                        Rouen
            Carentan   Bayeux Ouistreham
                  Saint-Lô Caen   Évreux
                              Falaise   PARIS
                  Avranches GERMAN SEVENTH ARMY
      Saint-Malo   Mortain

△ Radar
● German battery
★ Panzer Division
▨ Mines

of Britain, but the attack on Russia allowed only small numbers of troops to be left in the west. Hitler decided therefore to fortify the coastline only to the extent necessary to deter British landings, and the Canadians' defeat at Dieppe seemed to prove his calculations correct.

When America entered the war, however, Hitler redirected his attention to the construction of the "Atlantic Wall" against the new threat from the west.

Field Marshal Karl Gerd von Rundstedt was the supreme commander Hitler entrusted with the defense of a frontier of some 3100 miles, stretching from the North Sea to the Mediterranean. With no clear idea of where the Allies might decide to land, he was forced to give priority to certain sectors while virtually ignoring others. Construction of the Atlantic Wall—minefields, concrete walls, barbed-wire fences, and other deterrents—began in earnest in early 1942, the main focus being in the Pas-de-Calais region and around the major ports. Along the coast to the south of Calais, several heavy gun batteries capable of firing across the Channel were placed in massive concrete bunkers.

At sixty-nine, Field Marshal Karl Gerd von Rundstedt (left below) was the most senior of the German commanders. His post as Supreme Commander in the West was mainly honorific, as the important decisions were made by Hitler. Left: A German radar device on the French coast.

Along the coastline, in addition to the main artillery positions, were built hundreds of bunkers from which gunners were able to fire directly onto the beaches. Radar stations were also built, ostensibly to give German military headquarters early warning of an approaching enemy; in reality, the stations were not of much benefit, as their communications relied on easily sabotaged telephone wires. Nazi propaganda films

Below: A concrete seawall flanked by artillery mounted in concrete bunkers.

showed pictures of massive guns, giving the impression of impregnability, but in fact much of the Atlantic Wall was a sham.

Engineering for Overlord

Among the first priorities of the Allied planners was to develop artificial ports that could be assembled in England and towed across the Channel. A team formed of the most fertile brains in the construction industry soon devised an ingenious structure that came to be known as a mulberry harbor. The Allies decided to build two of these—one to support the American forces and one to support the British. Each was to be comprised of the following elements: First, a number of old ships were to be sunk off the French beaches to form breakwaters (called gooseberries), inside which vessels could anchor in calm water; second, a line of massive, six-hundred-ton concrete caissons (called phoenixes) were to be towed into position and sunk in a line to form a solid wall protecting the harbors; the final element consisted of a series of pontoons supporting lengths of floating roadway running from the piers onto the beaches. Construction of the various mulberry components had to be carried out under conditions of extreme secrecy and involved a

The PLUTO pipeline was a triumph of technology. Above left is one of the floating drums that carried the pipeline. As it was towed across the Channel, the pipe unrolled and sank to the seabed. Above right are pictured several of the concrete caissons that were towed across the Channel and flooded to form part of the ingenious mulberry harbors.

huge labor force of thousands of men housed in camps all along the south coast of England.

Another logistical puzzle for the planners was how to ensure an adequate supply of fuel to the mainland. The answer was provided by a project known as PLUTO (an acronym for "pipeline under the ocean"). Two versions were tested, one a flexible hollow cable and the other consisting of sections of metal pipe welded together. In August 1944, two pipelines of the flexible variety were laid across the Channel to Cherbourg to supply the Allied armies with much-needed gasoline and oil.

In addition, special tanks had to be designed to clear out bunkers and

Major General Percy Hobart, creator of the group of special types of tanks known as the "menagerie," was Montgomery's brother-in-law. In early 1943 he was given the job of developing methods of protecting the assault teams and engineers who would be forced to work on open beaches under enemy fire.

Examples of Specialist Armor

Opposite above: The "flying dustbin," a tank that could fire a large container of napalm. Opposite below: One of the weapons most feared by the German soldiers, the "crocodile" could direct a huge jet of flame into a bunker's firing slits. Above: The "bobbin" tank, which could unroll a strip of canvas over soft patches of sand. Left: A bobbin tank in action.

minefields, fill in anti-tank ditches, and position bridges. This assortment of "specialist armor" made a vital contribution to the overall success of D-Day.

Choosing the Commanders

The selection of the Supreme Commander of the Allied Expeditionary Force entailed a complicated exercise of political horse-trading between the Americans and the British. The powers eventually agreed on General Eisenhower, the brilliant and popular diplomat who had led Allied troops to a decisive victory in Africa. Eisenhower was

The senior Allied commanders in the Mediterranean: General Eisenhower (left), Air Chief Marshal Tedder (center), and General Alexander (right). Eisenhower would have preferred Alexander to Montgomery as ground forces commander during Overlord. As commander in chief in the Middle East, he had been Montgomery's superior. Tedder was in charge of the Allied air forces and Ike's deputy during Overlord. A flying ace from World War I, Tedder was given the job of coordinating the air and ground forces. By isolating the Normandy battlefields, Tedder's air force played a major role in the liberation of Europe. Examples of German bombers are shown above.

formally appointed by American President Franklin Delano Roosevelt in early December 1943. The selection of deputy supreme commander was British Air Chief Marshal Arthur W. Tedder, commander of the Allied air forces in the Mediterranean. For the post of naval commander, the natural candidate was the British Admiral Bertram H. Ramsay, who had planned the Torch landings. British Air Chief Marshal Trafford L. Leigh-Mallory was chosen as commander of the air forces.

The selection of a suitable ground commander, however, proved more difficult. Eisenhower's first choice was General Harold R. L. G. Alexander, but Churchill was adamant that this able British commander should remain in Italy. Instead, Montgomery was appointed. Commander of the British Eighth Army and in large part responsible for his sector's victory at El-Alamein, Montgomery was unquestionably the best man then available for the job, but questions regarding his personality were to lead to bitter contention in the future.

The Supreme Headquarters of the Allied Expeditionary Force, or SHAEF (which incorporated the COSSAC team), established itself in Britain to the west of London in early 1944 and expanded rapidly into a vast bureaucracy with ultimate authority and responsibility for the massive buildup of men and supplies. Operation Bolero, the movement of American troops into Britain, was soon in full swing, and the soldiers had to be housed, fed, and trained.

Montgomery arrived in Britain in January and found himself the inheritor of the original COSSAC Overlord plan, which he regarded as flawed in a number of respects. For instance, he saw right away that the front was far too narrow. He believed that the number of divisions to be landed should be increased from three to

Admiral Bertram Ramsay (below) first came to prominence when he masterminded the evacuation of British and French troops from Dunkirk in the summer of 1940. While naval commander in chief in the Mediterranean, he planned the Torch landings. His ships put a million men and their equipment ashore during Operation Neptune, the naval phase of Overlord.

A British X-class mini submarine (left). In addition to a crew of three, this vessel could accommodate two frogmen for beach reconnaissance missions. On the night of 17 January 1944, two swimmers landed at Vierville to investigate the sand on what was to become known as Omaha Beach. While they were working, a German sentry walked right past them, treading on the hand of one. Three days before D-Day, two such submarines submerged off the British beaches. At dawn on 6 June they came to the surface and activated radio beacons to guide in the landing craft.

five to permit an extension of the invasion to the west of the Vire River (Utah Beach), thus enabling Cherbourg to be captured more rapidly.

Deception and Intelligence Gathering: Operation Fortitude

Having decided upon the place of invasion, it became necessary to fool the Germans into believing that it would take place elsewhere. This subterfuge entailed a massive deception plan, code-named Operation Fortitude. The primary aim of the operation was to mask the arms buildup on the western end of England's south coast and concentrate German minds on the southeastern coast, opposite the Calais area. Enemy reconnaissance missions were "permitted" to penetrate the skies over Kent county, where they could photograph masses of "tanks" and "landing craft." The fact that these were actually inflatable rubber dummies, or made of plywood and canvas, was not apparent from the air, and the enemy intelligence authorities were effectively taken in.

Another component of the deception plan was the creation of a false headquarters known as the US 1st Army Group, apparently commanded by General George S. Patton, based in Kent and complete with fake radio traffic. The Germans knew of the American general's reputation as a fighting commander but were unaware of his true role, which was to take command of the US Third Army in Normandy during the breakout phase of the campaign. So successful were these measures that the Germans remained in ignorance of the true destination of Overlord until the actual bombardment started. And indeed, for some time after.

Below: A full-size inflatable Sherman tank carried by its "crew." This is just one example of the tremendous effort that was put into deceiving the enemy as to the whereabouts of the invasion. Teams of soldiers equipped with such devices and an air compressor moved around at night to create an illusion of troop concentrations opposite the Calais area. Overnight, small harbors would be filled with "landing craft," and fields with "airplanes." Expert set designers were recruited from theaters to create camouflage effects. The overwhelming success of the deception effort, Operation Fortitude, meant that the Allies' invasion of Normandy took the enemy completely by surprise.

No matter how good the military plan and how much is known about the enemy's activities, no army can fight a successful battle without first-class backup and support. For each soldier firing a rifle on the front line, there can be as many as seven others behind him, keeping him supplied with everything needed to maintain him in peak fighting condition.

CHAPTER II
PREPARING FOR THE INVASION

While von Rundstedt (right) enjoyed the luxury of his château outside Paris, all along the south coast of England, Allied troops practiced embarking and disembarking from their landing craft (opposite).

By January 1944 England's southern counties had been transformed into a vast military camp, and the buildup of the necessary forces and material for the invasion began to reach its climax. Pressed into service, the high-speed liners the *Queen Mary* and the *Queen Elizabeth,* each first having been repainted a drab gray color, transported thousands of American soldiers across the Atlantic. Nearly a million GIs were already packed into the rural landscapes around Somerset, Devon, and Dorset.

On the whole it was a peaceful "invasion," with little friction between the newcomers and the locals. Children loved the sticks of chewing gum and the chocolate bars that were freely handed out by the American GIs, and British women discovered the wonders of nylon stockings. England danced to the music of Glenn Miller, and numerous American expressions were absorbed into the everyday British language.

American, British, and Canadian armies were concentrated in the south and southeastern counties, with the latter using the huge meadows of Sussex Downs for their training. Hotels, guest houses, and schools were requisitioned for billeting, and the small harbors filled steadily with landing craft. To feed, house, supply, and

American officers having tea with a village vicar. This is one of many propaganda photographs taken to show that the "boys" were well-behaved.

give medical attention to such huge numbers, a complex organization had to be established almost from scratch. The unsung heroes of D-Day were the men and women who organized the logistics that made the invasion possible. There was no hope of glory or medals for these planners who toiled over endless lists of everything from tank engines to toilet paper, from French phrase books to complete mobile operating theaters.

American troops in battle uniform marching through an English village. The GIs were given a guidebook (inset) to teach them about England and the daily life and customs of the English people.

Training Needs

One of the planners' priorities was to find areas where the assault divisions could train realistically—using live ammunition and landing on beaches similar in topography to the ones they would encounter in Normandy. A number of coastal areas in the south of England were requisitioned, and their inhabitants—together with their household possessions and livestock—forced to move out. One such area was Slapton Sands, in south Devon, which was designated as an assault training zone for use mainly by

The Hershey bar was a hit with English children, who were unaccustomed to such luxuries. "Got any gum, chum?" became a popular phrase.

American forces. Eight villages were entirely evacuated by 20 September 1943, after which date all civilians were barred from reentry.

A vast and complex network of camps was established near the coast. Area A, to the north of Portsmouth, consisted of over forty-three miles of parking areas for tanks and other vehicles and seventeen barbed-wire–encircled camps. (Once inside the camps, the assault formations were briefed on their destination, and any further communication with the outside world was forbidden.) To accommodate the training and supply of the troops, huge supply depots were built,

One of the most important factors in ensuring the success of the landings was adequate training. Here (left and opposite below), soldiers practice unarmed combat. Large areas of the English countryside were reserved for maneuvers and firing ranges. Conditions were made as realistic as possible, and the inter-action between infantry, armored units, and air support was carefully coordinated. There were also endless rehearsals of getting men and

vehicles on and off landing craft in the right order. Even such simple matters as waterproofing rifles had to be learned. For certain units with specific missions— such as the capture of a German gun position—full-scale models of the target were built, complete with dummy bunkers and trenches.

the narrow English roads widened, bridges strengthened, and hundreds of miles of new railroad constructed.

The tabulation and organization of the loading plans for individual landing craft and ships—each of which

Supply services worked around the clock to stockpile vehicles and equipment, organize rail transport, and build supply depots.

had to deliver the right men and supplies to the right place in the proper order—was an additional complex undertaking. An assault formation was a finely balanced entity that included infantry, armored support vehicles, signalers, demolition engineers, and medical teams. And once the assault formations were ashore and moving inland, the second wave had to arrive bringing more ammunition and vehicles, spare parts, fuel, rations, artillery, and even the battalion cooks. Returning craft would be filled with the wounded, prisoners of war, and damaged vehicles.

Fine Tuning

"Y-Day," set for 1 June, was the date when everything had to be ready to go, awaiting only the supreme commander's word. After Y-Day no further corrections could be made to the master plan. This key date was revealed to a select audience consisting of the general staff, the senior planners, and the actual assault commanders (down to the divisional level) at the headquarters of the British 21st Army Group, at St. Paul's

The faces of the Allied high command (from left to right, Bradley, Ramsay, Tedder, Eisenhower, Montgomery, Leigh-Mallory, and Bedell Smith) here radiate unity of purpose, yet their later quarrels were to cast a shadow over operations in Normandy.

School in London, on 15 May. Also present were King George VI and Winston Churchill. At the end of the proceedings, General Eisenhower is said to have remarked, "Hitler has missed his one and only chance of destroying with a single well-aimed bomb the entire high command of the Allied forces."

Seated on hard school benches, the dignitaries faced a huge map spread across the opposite wall. There remained only three weeks before the invasion, and little was left for the senior commanders to do besides carry out a strenuous program of visits to the assault formations and follow-up echelons. Both Montgomery and Eisenhower made a point of personally speaking to as many of the men as possible, to "binge" them up (to borrow one of Montgomery's favorite expressions).

While these visits were being carried out, SHAEF and the 21st Army Group were on the move to the countryside of Hampshire, just north of Portsmouth. There they set up camp in and around Southwick House, a large mansion that had been requisitioned for Eisenhower's staff. It was at Southwick House that the decision to launch Operation Neptune, the first, naval phase of Overlord, would be made.

French General Pierre-Joseph Koenig (above) was appointed to command all of the various factions of the French Resistance that would help the Allies in France. The Allied planners harbored a fear that units of the Resistance with differing political opinions might end up fighting each other instead of the Germans.

Military Exercises

As many of the assault units lacked combat experience, a number of realistic exercises were carried out. These exercises, usually performed with live ammunition, included shore bombardment by warships and aircraft maneuvers. One such rehearsal was Exercise Tiger,

Night after night, converted bomber aircraft flew from England to France by moonlight with their cargoes of arms, ammunition, and explosives. On the ground, tense groups of men and women—members of the Resistance—waited for the noise of the engines. When they sighted the ghostly shapes of the parachutes, they rushed to the drop sites to collect the containers and move them to safety before daylight.

SABOT

conducted at the end of April. The practice assault entailed a landing of the US 4th Infantry Division on Slapton Sands in Devon, followed by an advance inland to meet the two American airborne divisions, the 101st and the 82nd. In all, twenty-five thousand men and 2750 vehicles had to be moved, landed, and then recovered after the three-day maneuver.

Purely by chance, a group of German E-boats (surface torpedo boats) from Cherbourg stumbled on one of the convoys approaching the practice area. The enemy managed to sink two LSTs (specially designed landing vessels for tanks and trucks) and severely damage three others before making off, causing nearly seven hundred American

Using explosives placed under the rails—preferably on a curve, which was more difficult to repair—the French resisters destroyed strategic sections of railway lines (opposite).

casualties. There ensued a fearful panic in case any personnel with knowledge of the invasion plan had been fished out of the water and taken prisoner by the enemy.

As an exercise, Tiger was a complete failure. The medical services proved incapable of moving "casualties" back to the beach, and communications systems collapsed. The commander of the engineer assault battalion was dismissed on the spot.

A few days later, Exercise Fabius was mounted, with simulated landings carried out at various points along the south coast of England. Fortunately, this exercise proved to be generally satisfactory, and ground officers were able to iron out details as well as become acquainted with the naval personnel who would transport them on the big day.

Suitcase-sized transmitting/receiving radios were supplied to the Resistance networks together with trained operators, known as "pianists." Theirs was one of the most hazardous jobs, as German intelligence teams could soon locate their positions with detection devices.

The "Sausage Machine"

The "sausage machine" was the nickname given to the marshaling system into which the men of the assault units were fed during the month of May, not to emerge again until the orders to embark were given. All of the southern and much of the eastern coast of England had been declared off limits, and travel into and out of the region—except for very urgent reasons—was banned. The marshaling camps, surrounded with barbed wire and guarded by armed sentries, penned in the men who were gradually briefed but not told their actual destination. Plainclothes intelligence personnel moved around the area listening and watching for

Field Marshal Rommel (below) making a tour of inspection along the Normandy coast. He personally supervised much of the construction of Hitler's "Atlantic Wall." Owing to shortages of material and manpower, however, many of the planned obstacles were unfinished when the Allies landed.

A meeting of the German high command at the Hotel Prince of Wales in Paris on 8 May 1944. From left to right: Commander of the Panzer Group West, General Schweppenburg; General Blaskowitz, commander of Army Group G; Field Marshal Sperrle, the Luftwaffe (the German air force) commander in chief; von Rundstedt; Rommel; and, representing the Kriegsmarine (the German navy), Admiral Kranke.

signs of people talking too much. The invasion preparations could not be hidden from the local civilian population, of course, and security authorities were desperately worried about German spies and possible information leaks.

In this final period there was much work to be done. All vehicles had to be waterproofed, and weapons—especially the new tanks—had to be test-fired and have their sights set. Supplies had to be stockpiled in the right places, and the follow-up divisions had to be ready to move south as soon as the assault divisions had moved out. Each single division on the battlefield—up to fifteen thousand men—required six hundred tons of supplies per day.

But, like a vast mosaic, everything gradually fell into place. Even adequate supplies of condoms—to put over the ends of rifle barrels to keep them dry—were found. From distant harbors in Scotland, the slow-moving old ships that would form the gooseberry breakwaters commenced their final voyage. As a final precaution before the actual operations began, two X-class miniature submarines slipped silently out of

Below: A German bunker in Normandy camouflaged as a typical vacation home.

Portsmouth and headed for the coast of Normandy. There they were to lie submerged on the seabed until the invasion fleets approached, at which time they would rise to the surface and activate radio beacons to mark the boundaries of the landings.

The Allies Worked Closely with the Varied Factions of the French Resistance

The French Resistance reflected all of the country's political divisions—there were Gaullist and Communist groups as well as those with monarchist leanings and others loyal to the dissolved French army. Responsibility for supplying the resisters was largely in the hands of the British SOE (Special Operations Executive), but a few weeks before D-Day, General Pierre-Joseph Koenig was named head of the FFI (Forces Françaises de l'Interieur, or "Free French Forces of the Interior"), in an effort to provide some level of coordination between the various factions.

Resisters in the Normandy region had been ordered by the Allies to keep a low profile, collect intelligence, and not provoke any violent reprisals. Their job during the invasion would be to slow the movement of German armored divisions into the battle area. To train and arm the resisters, a large number of missions were dropped all over France, each consisting of two uniformed officers, either British or American, accompanied by a radio operator. These teams were backed up by several groups of men from the Special Air Service Regiment who were parachuted in with their jeeps to harry enemy lines of communication in the interior of France.

Night after night during the months before D-Day, torches were lit in secluded fields all over France when the watchers heard the drone of the approaching aircraft. Then, floating down through the darkness, would come the parachutes—bringing arms, explosives, and sometimes men to lead and train the daring

The "landing ship, tank" (LST, above right) was a large ocean-going vessel. Its smaller counterpart, the "landing craft, tank" (LCT, above left) had a flat bottom and could run directly onto a beach to unload the tanks.

patriots. All over the country, small parties of patriotic French men and women began to sabotage the German war effort, often suffering terrible losses in the process. Railways were destroyed, bridges demolished, telephone lines cut, and German officers assassinated. Locations of suitable bombing targets were radioed back to London. Eisenhower later stated that such activities shortened the war in Europe by nine months.

The various pockets of the Resistance were given instructions from Allied planners by means of messages broadcast by BBC Radio in London. These usually took the form of two lines of a well-known poem. When the first line was broadcast, it meant that invasion was imminent and that the recipients should be prepared. When the second line was heard, resisters knew to go into action.

This American LST (below) was badly damaged by torpedo fire from German E-boats during Exercise Tiger.

A British officer showing paratroopers their landing sites on a map that, for security purposes, has no place-names (opposite).

Overleaf: Allied troops embarking at Weymouth (above) and German soldiers stationed along the Atlantic Wall (below).

The German Army Suffered from an Unwieldy Command Structure and Conflicting Personalities

The arrival of German Field Marshal Erwin Rommel as commander of German Army Group B in early January sparked off a flurry of activity along the occupied coastline, as the enemy troops were put to work constructing extra beach defenses, flooding low-lying areas, and planting sharpened stakes (known as Rommel's asparagus) in fields to hinder the landing of gliders. Enormous numbers of mines were laid, extra pillboxes built, and pre-war fortifications pillaged for such items as bulletproof doors. Luckily for the Allies, the Germans were severely hampered by lack of troops and supplies and were unable to complete all the measures that the energetic field marshal demanded.

Rommel was convinced that the only way to defeat an Allied landing was to do so before it could establish itself —in other words, on the beaches. Aware as he was of the Allies' air superiority, he realized how difficult it would be to move reserves to the battle front once a successful landing had been made. To that end, he argued that the available armored divisions should be stationed near the coast in order to hit an invasion force as soon as possible.

His superior, however, the elderly von Rundstedt, held the opposite view: He believed that a strong central pool of armored divisions should be kept well back from the front and then used for a decisive counterattack. In this he was supported by General Geyr von Schweppenburg, commander of the Panzer Group West. (A German

The faces of these American GIs waiting to leave for France (below) show the strain imposed by months of training and uncertainty about what awaited them on the other side of the Channel.

panzer division was roughly equivalent to an Allied armored division.)

Their argument raged throughout the spring of 1944, and naturally Hitler was deeply involved. He decided to form a reserve of four armored divisions under his own control and to station them in the vicinity of Paris. Thus, Rommel was left with only three such divisions to cover the entire coast between the Schelde River, in Belgium,

Admiral Ramsay's headquarters for Operation Neptune at Norfolk House in London (below). Members of the WRNS (Women's Royal Navy Service) are assisting.

and the Loire River, in central France—a stretch of nearly eight hundred miles. Although he personally was convinced of the possibility of an Allied landing in Normandy, he left two of his panzer divisions north of the Seine and only one, the 21st Panzer, to the south, near Caen. Its presence there, however, proved decisive in the Allies' failure to capture that city on D-Day.

Many of the divisions manning Normandy's coastal defenses were low-grade units filled with elderly reservists and those who were otherwise generally unfit. Other units consisted of foreign prisoners—Russians, Ukrainians, Cossacks, and Tartars—who had "volunteered" for service in the German army. Many of the German artillery pieces were captured weapons and lacked standard ammunition. These drawbacks were deemed unimportant, however, as almost all the senior German commanders remained convinced that the actual invasion would be to the north of the Seine, in the Pas-de-Calais area.

When to Land?

Eisenhower described the parameters of the landing as follows: "We wanted to cross the Channel with our convoys at night so that darkness would conceal the strength and direction of our several attacks. We wanted a moon for our airborne assaults. We needed approximately forty minutes of daylight preceding the ground assault to complete our bombing and preparatory bombardment. We had to attack on a relatively low tide because of beach obstacles which had to be removed while uncovered." In June, such conditions were available only between the fifth and seventh days of the month.

Embarkation of men and equipment began on 2 June, but on 4 June a powerful storm—the worst in twenty years—lashed the south coast of England. At the regular briefings at Southwick House, it was the chief meteorologist, Group

Captain James M. Stagg of the Royal Air Force, who was listened to most attentively, although the weight of the ultimate decision rested solely on Eisenhower's shoulders.

Early in the morning of 4 June, Eisenhower ordered a twenty-four-hour postponement, which meant an uncomfortable period for the men waiting in the flat-bottomed landing ships. Later in the day, Stagg was able to announce that there would be a brief letup in the weather on 6 June. The final weather conference was held at 0400 hours on Monday. At exactly 0415 hours, Ike, after listening to the opinions of the other senior commanders, spoke the now-famous words, "O.K. Let's go."

The Departure

In Shoreham, Southampton, Portsmouth, Portland, and Plymouth, as well as many other smaller harbors on

Tightly packed landing craft along the Southampton docks (above).

Once he had made the final decision to launch Overlord, Ike had little to do. On the evening of 5 June, he called for his car and drove to the airfield where the men of the US 101st Airborne Division were preparing to leave (opposite). "I stayed with them until the last of them were in the air, somewhere around midnight."

General Montgomery—who, in spite of his abrasive style, inspired great loyalty among those reporting to him—briefs his headquarters staff in a field before they depart for Normandy (left).

England's south coast, the landing craft were packed so tightly that there was hardly any room left to maneuver. Along every road leading south, columns of vehicles moved nose to tail past curious civilians going about their normal lives. Churchill traveled on his special train to be near the action, and only Eisenhower's firm remonstrances and the king's wily arguments kept him from setting off for France on D-Day on board a destroyer.

Units of the assault fleet began to leave Southampton during the afternoon of 5 June, while those coming from further west had been at sea since the early morning. The inhabitants of the small port of Salcombe, which had been home to a flotilla of American landing craft, woke to find their harbor totally empty. Every ship was heading for a rendezvous point just to the south of the Isle of Wight, from which all the various convoys would then turn toward France.

American soldiers and vehicles aboard a landing vessel (below).

On board the heaving vessels, commanding officers opened sealed envelopes as soon as they passed the outer defenses of the harbors. In them they found the maps that named their true destinations—a crucial piece of information that had been kept from them until this point for reasons of security. On the larger ships were held church services, during which will forms were handed out to the attentive congregations. Many of the participants later wrote of a sense of unreality as they sailed into battle through the night, completely powerless in the capable hands of the sailors.

On the Continent

Convinced that an invasion was unlikely, given the appalling weather conditions, Field Marshal Rommel left France in his staff car for a few days at home in southern Germany. In fact, many German officers were absent from their command posts on the night of 5 June, several attending a war game in the town of Rennes, in Brittany.

After the main BBC news that night, a stream of two-line poems was transmitted, and, in the darkness, men and women of the Resistance slipped out to fulfill their

Late in the evening of 5 June, American and British airborne paratroopers climbed aboard their transport aircraft (below) and left from airfields to the northwest of London. The main type of aircraft used was the American DC3 "Dakota."

small but crucial roles in Overlord. A young woman who worked in the post office of a small coastal village wrecked the telephone exchange before locking up and going home for the night. As she rode off on her bicycle she saw some German soldiers shooting at targets on the beach. "You will be the targets tomorrow," she must have thought.

As dusk fell, the airborne troops gathered their equipment together and made their way to the waiting airplanes and gliders parked wingtip to wingtip on dozens of airfields. Eisenhower joked and chatted with the men of the 101st Airborne in the darkness, just the whites of their eyes showing through the camouflage cream on their faces. The first to leave was a group from the British 22nd Independent Parachute Company, whose task it was to find the drop zones and mark them with flares and radio beacons.

After everything else, the final component of the deception operation was put to sea. A group of motor launches equipped with radar devices simulating a much larger force headed north up the Channel, ostensibly for a landing site between Dieppe and Boulogne.

Two of Overlord's most important figures were destined to wait on the sidelines. Churchill (below left), who had planned to sail with the fleet on D-Day, was requested not to do so by the king. Eisenhower (below right), waiting impatiently at his headquarters for the first news to arrive, finally went to bed with a book.

The fleet of troop-carrying aircraft were the first away, heading for drop zones on Cotentin Peninsula. They flew in from the west over the Channel Islands, in an attempt to skirt the heavy concentration of anti-aircraft fire based around Cherbourg. Even so, there was enough flak to unnerve many of the less experienced pilots.

CHAPTER III
THE LANDINGS: 6 JUNE 1944

As dawn broke on 6 June, German sentries looking out to sea from their bunkers saw that the horizon was black with ships. Alarm bells rang, and sleepy men tumbled from their bunks. Soon they would be fighting for their lives as the landing craft disgorged men and tanks under a hail of fire.

The US 82nd Airborne Division was due to drop near the small town of Sainte-Mère-Eglise, on Cotentin Peninsula, at 0100 hours on the morning of 6 June. But many of the paratroopers missed their targets and were scattered all over the countryside, losing most of their equipment in the process. Members of the US 101st Airborne suffered equally badly. Their mission was to drop inland of the flooded area behind Utah Beach to secure the exit roads and key bridges at Carentan, a town in the peninsula's center, but many of the men were inadvertently dropped into the water and drowned.

Officers found it impossible to rally cohesive bodies of men, and a series of small battles erupted all over the area as the enemy began to react. Disaster appeared imminent, but the sheer determination of the young American troops slowly paid off as they regrouped and made their way toward the battle. Ironically, the widely scattered drops caused confusion in the various German headquarters. So many telephone lines had been cut by French Resistance workers that the incoming reports failed to give a cohesive picture and the German corps commander was unable to take full control of the battle.

From midnight on, wave after wave of Dakotas flew over Cotentin Peninsula, and paratroopers floated down into the dark countryside. In spite of their wide dispersal, enough men gathered to form a cohesive perimeter and repel the strong German counterattacks. General Matthew Ridgway, commander of the US 82nd Airborne Division, set up his first headquarters in an orchard. He later wrote, "The Germans were all around us, of course, sometimes within five hundred yards of my command post, but in the fierce and confused fighting that was going on all about, they did not launch the strong attack that could have wiped out our eggshell perimeter defense."

Airborne Operations—British

Simultaneous to the American landings, the British 6th Airborne Division landed to the east of Caen,

The insignias of the US airborne divisions: The 82nd (top) and the 101st (bottom). Hundreds of plywood gliders (left) were towed across the Channel and then released to glide down into the fields. Although many crashed, others landed safely and were able to deliver their loads.

intending to secure crossings over the Orne River. One of the leading formations was a detachment of six gliders, under the command of Major John Howard, whose extremely difficult and hazardous mission was to capture two bridges—one over the Orne and the other over a canal at Bénouville, a few miles north of Caen. Once released from the towing aircraft, the gliders swooped down silently in the dark, somehow managing to land in exactly the targeted

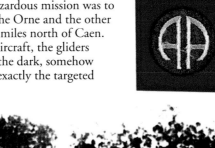

place. Faces blackened, the daring paratroopers swarmed out and, in spite of some opposition, succeeded in overwhelming the German defenders.

The rest of the division dropped to the east of the Orne, and although a number of men drowned in the marshy areas near the river, a firm defense perimeter was established. Engineers demolished the fields of "Rommel's asparagus," enabling the gliders to land with vehicles, light artillery, and other weapons that would be needed before the night was over. At 0300 hours, as the men

Above: An aerial photograph of the Merville battery after it had been bombed. Below: The wreckage of a glider.

frantically worked, they heard the fleets of bombers roaring overhead to deliver thousands of tons of bombs onto the coastal defenses, followed at 0500 hours by the guns of the warships signaling the arrival of the invasion fleet.

Although advance units of the 21st Panzer Division were in the area, their commander was away in Paris. In the confusion, no orders were issued for the division to attack until much later in the morning, by which time the chance to wipe out the fragile bridgehead established by the British had been lost.

The presence of a huge assembly of ships off the coast of Normandy was picked up by German coastal radar, which duly reported its position, but—luckily for the assault forces—no general alert was issued to the shore defenses. At 0500 hours the bombardment vessels opened fire on precisely defined targets and, as soon as light permitted, spotter aircraft checked the accuracy of the guns. No enemy aircraft appeared, and the only interference was from a small force of E-boats, which was easily beaten off.

Assault on the Beaches

Protected by the warships, the assault formations lined up for the approach onto the beaches. This was performed like a complicated ballet movement on the rough seas. Motor launches acting as marshaling controllers marked the

While Allied aircraft dropped their bombs on the enemy's defenses, the Allied naval bombardment force moved into position. Each ship had a specific target—a coastal battery or stronghold—and, above the fleet, aircraft spotted the accuracy of the firing. Huge shells rained down on the defenders while the troops in the assault wave scrambled into their landing craft. The warships remained in position until the battle moved inland and out of range. An Allied battleship is shown below.

start of the run-in on each flank. Farthest out to sea, the converted ships carrying the bulk of the infantry hove to and lowered the small LCAs (short for "landing craft, assault") into which the heavily laden troops had to scramble, climbing down nets and canvas chutes. All the various types of landing vessels then had to line up in a precise order so that each element was in the right position. The entire assemblage was guarded by a fleet of destroyers on each flank. The following is a description of a typical line-up: In the lead went the LCS(M)s (landing craft support, medium) with forward artillery spotters to direct gunfire onto targets among the beach

As shells from the warships screamed past, it seemed to the seasick men watching aboard the landing craft that the whole beach was on fire (above).

defenses. Behind them came the amphibious, propeller-driven DD, or "dual-drive," tanks. These were followed by a line of LCTs (landing craft, tank) loaded with specialist armor and, finally, the infantry in the LCAs. Accompanying the assault waves were support landing craft armed with anti-aircraft guns to deter enemy planes and rocket-firing craft to saturate the defenses.

For many of the men, tortured by seasickness, the prospect of finally going ashore—even if into battle—was preferable to remaining at sea. They were comforted by the sound of waves of bombers roaring overhead and the continuous firing from the warships.

Utah Beach

Today the gently sloping stretch of seashore known as Utah Beach is a paradise for vacationers, with only the vestiges of concrete bunkers to remind them of the events of D-Day. That June morning, however, the beach was completely obscured by smoke from the bombardment, and thirty thousand men and thirty-five hundred vehicles were assembling offshore, waiting for dawn. The weather was grim, with low scudding clouds and a rough sea whipped up by an offshore breeze.

The actual landing was spearheaded by two squadrons of DD tanks, which had been successfully launched two miles offshore in sheltered water. As they lumbered onto the beach they dropped their rubber "skirts" and opened

General Hobart and his team created the DD (dual-drive) tank by fitting standard Sherman tanks with twin propellers. Rubberized canvas "skirts" allowed the thirty-three-ton tanks to float. Once ashore, the

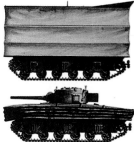

skirts were dropped and the tanks could operate normally. On D-Day many were launched too far out to sea and sank with their crews before they could reach the land.

US 82ND AIRBORNE DIVISION
0130 hrs.
SAINTE-MÈRE-ÉGLISE

LES FORGES

SAINT-MARTIN-
DE-VARREVILLE

flooded zones

anti-tank ditch   *stronghold*

SWORD •Ouistreham
       •Bernières
  JUNO GOLD •Vierville-sur-Mer
              Pointe-du-Hoc
       OMAHA   UTAH•

US 4TH INFANTRY
DIVISION

Il faut sans délai vous éloigner, avec votre famille, pendant quelques jours, de la zone de danger où vous vous trouvez.

N'encombrez pas les routes.   Dispersez-vous dans la campagne, autant que possible.

PARTEZ SUR LE CHAMP !
VOUS N'AVEZ PAS UNE MINUTE A PERDRE !

fire on the surprised Germans. Behind them, the first waves of the US 4th Infantry Division were landed at low tide, when the water level was well below the beach obstacles. Although the soldiers had to cross more than five hundred yards of open beach to reach the dunes, return fire was only sporadic. As they and the tanks cleared out the enemy bunkers, teams of engineers demolished as many of the obstacles as they could before the rising tide covered them.

Although there was fighting around some of the German strongholds, the infantry soon began to move off across the causeways over the flooded lagoon and, by 1300 hours, had met up with men from the US 101st Airborne Division. By nightfall, a solid bridgehead had been established and was being held firmly against random and

Part of General Eisenhower's message to the inhabitants of Normandy (above).

American commanders watch the events of D-Day from aboard the USS *Augusta*. From left to right: Rear Admiral Alan R. Kirk, the naval task force commander; General Omar N. Bradley; Brigadier General William B. Kean; and Rear Admiral Arthur Dewey Struble (with binoculars).

Once the beachhead had been established and the engineers had blown passages through the obstacles on the shore, tank landings were able to unload their cargoes directly onto the beaches. Many, however, were disabled by enemy fire, and their wrecks added to the chaos along the water's edge. As more and more landing craft arrived, vehicles of all types, unable to move off, remained jammed there. The hero of Utah Beach was fifty-seven-year-old Brigadier General Theodore Roosevelt, Jr. (son of former US President Theodore Roosevelt), who calmly directed the traffic.

uncoordinated German attacks. By far the worst problem was the congestion on the beach, owing to the restricted exits. As succeeding waves of infantry and armor landed they had to be moved off as quickly as possible—often directly into the line of fire—to make room for the supplies and heavy equipment that followed.

On board the USS *Augusta,* waiting just off the beaches, was General Omar N. Bradley. The commander of the US First Army was satisfied by the reports he was receiving from Utah Beach, but was deeply disturbed by events further to the east.

Omaha Beach

Omaha Beach is about three miles long and is overlooked by high cliffs. The only exits are up the steep ravines at each end that lead to villages of solidly built stone houses. Along the actual beach runs a ten-foot-high concrete seawall atop which one can still see the concrete emplacements that housed the Germans' 88-mm guns. It was a perfect defensive position.

The assault regiments from the US 1st and 29th infantry divisions had a long and difficult approach to Omaha—nearly ten miles through storm-lashed seas—

Small teams of heroic medical orderlies did their best to care for the many wounded scattered along the shoreline (below left). Many other injured men drowned when the tide came in.

and were obliged to attack without the promised armored support. (Due to the risky water conditions, one of the two battalions of DD tanks was not launched offshore, as had been planned. Of the twenty-nine tanks from the battalion that was launched, some sank like stones and the others were swamped by water pouring over their "skirts." Only two tanks reached the beach intact.)

Low clouds obscured the aerial bombers' targets, and smoke made it difficult for warships to spot theirs, with the result that the defenses were both intact and wide-awake as the first wave of landing craft came into view through the haze. The vessels were met by a barrage of shells, mortar bombs, and machine-gun fire. Two of the first six craft on one beach sector alone were sunk, while others ran aground on an offshore sandbank, forcing the men to wade through water up to their shoulders. Many soldiers were shot, and many others drowned. Small units did manage to move off the beach, but all pretense of cohesion was abandoned. As successive waves of men and equipment poured onto the killing field of Omaha Beach, it was clogged by vehicles that were unable to move. So bad were the conditions at 0915 hours that Bradley seriously considered abandoning the landing and rerouting the remaining men through one of the British beaches.

The body of a slain GI lies amid the debris of Omaha Beach, while other soldiers run for cover (below). Within minutes, all semblance of cohesion had been lost, and the enemy poured down a hail of mortar and machine-gun fire on the exposed attackers.

"As the morning lengthened, my worries deepened.... From [the] messages we could piece together only an incoherent account of sinkings, swampings, heavy enemy fire, and chaos on the beaches."
Omar N. Bradley
A Soldier's Story
1951

Rather than any grand concept, it was sheer courage and basic survival instinct on the part of individuals and small groups of men that saved the day. By early afternoon, more tanks had been landed directly onto the beach, although the exits were still open only to those on foot, who had to pick their way through the extensive minefields in single file. But by nightfall the US 1st Infantry Division had gained a tenuous hold on the road that ran inland behind the beach and vehicles were starting to move through the exits. A less experienced unit than the "Big Red One" (the famous moniker of the US 1st Infantry Division, taken from their divisional

NING EDITION

cisco Chronicle

SION!

insignia) would almost certainly have been defeated that morning. The fact that they were not is a dramatic demonstration of the determination and bravery of the American troops.

A group of US Rangers—soldiers specially trained for close-range fighting—attacked the heavy coastal battery, situated at Pointe-du-Hoc, on top of the high cliffs above the beach. Landing at the base of the cliffs, the Rangers were for a time pinned down on a narrow strip of beach until an Allied destroyer shelled the defenders. The Rangers then had to scale the cliffs while Germans fired at them from above. Those who made it to the top engaged in bitter hand-to-hand combat around the stronghold, only to discover that the Germans had earlier removed the feared guns from the bunkers to an open field further inland. Constantly counterattacked, the Rangers nevertheless managed to hold the position through the night.

Gold Beach

Gold Beach was the responsibility of the British 50th Northumbrian Division and the 8th Armored Brigade. Accompanying them was a Royal Marine Commando unit, whose task was to swing west and seize the nearby town of Arromanches as a base for the British mulberry harbor.

The weather at the launch site was appalling, and here—as at Omaha—it was decided not to launch the DD

The US 2nd Ranger Battalion was given the task of scaling the hundred-foot-high cliffs above Omaha and eliminating the strong German battery emplaced there in concrete bunkers. The six 155-mm howitzers could have fired on Omaha Beach with deadly effect. After a preliminary bombing raid at 0430 hours, two companies landed on the rocks at the base of the cliffs. In an action reminiscent of a medieval attack on a castle, the Rangers fired rocket-propelled hooks attached to ropes up the cliffs. As the men started to climb, the Germans tried to cut the ropes and dropped grenades on the attackers' heads. Meanwhile, a US destroyer that had moved close to shore fired at the enemy from close range. One by one the surviving Rangers reached the top, only to discover that there were no guns in the bunkers after all. They had been moved to a nearby open field.

At left, the American flag flies over the captured blockhouse at Pointe-du-Hoc.

tanks out at sea, but rather to land them directly behind the infantry. The assault wave managed to land clear of the beach obstacles, but the stiff wind buffeting up the tide meant that the mines became obscured more quickly than expected—and thus were less easily cleared by the engineers. Successive waves of landing craft had to pick passages through the explosive beach debris,

Paintings like the one above give an illusion of the battles on the beaches. More realistic is the photograph below, showing heavily laden British soldiers lining up for the move inland.

and many vessels were damaged in the process.

The battle of Gold Beach, however, was won with the aid of the specialist armor that landed ahead of the infantry and the amphibious tanks that landed behind. By afternoon, Arromanches had been secured and the British soldiers were marching inland toward Bayeux.

Juno Beach

Juno Beach stretches along either side of the small fishing port of Courseulles, several miles east of Arromanches. Beyond its dunes lay a number of coastal villages that had been fortified by the Germans. Juno was assigned to the men of the Canadian 3rd Division, who were thirsting to avenge their losses at Dieppe.

The main hazard at Juno was the presence of offshore reefs, which forced the assault wave to land later in the morning, when the water had already covered most of the obstacles. Since the engineers were unable to clear paths through the submerged obstacles, many of the first landing craft were blown up by the mines.

In spite of a preliminary aerial bombardment, there were enough determined Germans holed up in the seafront houses to pour a withering fire onto the beaches as the Canadians dashed for cover. The arrival of specialist armor was delayed in many sectors of the beach, which hindered the clearing of the exits. As wave after wave of vehicles and tanks were landed, they had to pick their way through the tangle of wrecked landing craft along the high-tide mark.

The Canadians had a hard fight at Saint-Aubin, where they had to harry the Germans out of the underground passages of a concrete stronghold, but by evening a solid bridgehead—linking the Canadians with the British XXX Corps from Gold Beach—had been established. As the battle died down, civilians emerged from their cellars to offer carefully hoarded bottles of strong drink to the exhausted and thirsty Canadians—many of whom were of French origin.

B elow are pictured two types of obstacles placed on the beaches by Rommel's troops. In the foreground, affixed to the top of a metal post, is an anti-tank mine designed to detonate if hit by a landing craft. In the background is a spiked tetrahedron, or "hedgehog," for ripping open the thin skins of boats.

Sword Beach

Sword Beach was assaulted by the British 3rd Infantry Division and its supporting units, including a force of French Commandos serving with the Scottish 1st Commando Brigade. The Commandos were to clear a way through the town of Ouistreham, very near Bénouville, and then meet the members of the British 6th Airborne Division who were waiting at the Orne bridgehead.

After a massive preliminary bombardment, the heaviest on any of the beaches that day,

Scottish Brigadier Lord Lovat led the 1st Commando Brigade ashore at Ouistreham. This photograph (left) was taken in the summer of 1942, on his return to England from the disastrous Dieppe raid.

the DD tanks were launched. In spite of the heavy seas, most of them reached the shore, closely followed by the LCTs loaded with specialist armored vehicles. Close on their heels came the infantry—accompanied by bagpiper Bill Millin. (Millin was the personal bagpiper of Scotsman Lord Lovat, also known as Simon Fraser, the twenty-fifth chief of the Fraser clan and commander of the 1st Brigade.)

At Ouistreham, the assaulting troops were faced by a solid line of enemy-held seafront villas—even a casino that the Germans had turned into a fortress. But they quickly set about storming the houses one by one, and soon the first groups of gray-clad German prisoners were stumbling back toward the shore with their hands above their heads.

Having made short work of the fortified casino and the town of Ouistreham, Lord Lovat and his men then broke out into open country and began their march toward the bridges over the Orne and the Bénouville canal. They fought their way through light opposition, but on arrival at the bridgehead became entangled in the battle between the British 6th Airborne and the newly arrived 21st Panzer Division.

Commander Philippe Kieffer led a unit of French Commandos that assisted Lord Lovat and his men at Ouistreham.

The first German prisoners being marched along the beach at Ouistreham to board the recently emptied landing craft that would take them back to England (left).

Counterattacks and Consolidation of the Beachhead

By midday, Hitler's Atlantic Wall had been seriously breached, although the Allies' toehold was still precarious. The landing of follow-up units on the beaches was severely hampered by both the weather and the lack of exits for such heavy traffic. Nonetheless, there was an enormous sense of relief back at the various headquarters in America and England that losses, while significant, had not been as heavy as feared. General Eisenhower, powerless to intervene actively, had to content himself with reading reports as they came in to Southwick House. When news of the disaster at Omaha arrived, those waiting with him

By the evening of D-Day, the Americans had managed to consolidate a slender bridgehead inland from Omaha Beach (above)—which remained congested with vehicles and wreckage—while follow-up units waited at sea.

The chance absence of Rommel on D-Day added to the confusion in the German chain of command. He was told of the invasion by a telephone call late in the morning to his home in Germany. He departed for France immediately but did not reach his headquarters until late afternoon. Rommel's beach obstacles had failed to hinder the landings in any appreciable way, and he lacked the mobile reserves he needed to carry out his plan of defeating the Allies before they could consolidate a bridgehead.

Panther tanks of the 21st Panzer Division parked among the trees (below). Stationed to the south and east of Caen, the 21st Panzer Division was the only mobile unit capable of a decisive counterattack. However, Rommel had issued orders that the division was not to intervene in the case of enemy landings without orders from his headquarters. By the end of D-Day, the Allies had destroyed a quarter of the 21st Panzer's armor.

could see the terrible strain he was under.

As a direct result of their tangled chain of command, the Germans had lost the initiative. Rommel, who might have been able to galvanize the German troops, did not return from Germany until late in the afternoon of D-Day. Von Rundstedt, for his part, remained convinced that the landings in Normandy were a diversion and that the main assault would come later in the Calais area—a view that was shared by the Wehrmacht (Germany army) high command. Although there were two armored divisions within striking distance of Normandy—the Panzer Lehr Division and the 12th SS Panzer ("SS"

standing for *Schutzstaffel,* the elite corps)—neither could be moved without the direct permission of Hitler, who was fast asleep at his villa in Berchtesgaden, in southeastern Bavaria. It was midday before he became aware of the situation and reluctantly gave permission for the two divisions to move. When they did so, in the late afternoon, they were immediately harried by Allied fighter-bombers.

The one formation that was readily available, the 21st Panzer commanded by Major General Edgar Feuchtinger, was largely paralyzed by having first received no orders, then contradictory ones. Aware of the British 6th Airborne bridgehead, which was being attacked by one of his units, Feuchtinger had decided to mount a general assault, only to be told to concentrate his tanks on the other side of the Orne. It was not until late afternoon that his forces were in position to check the belated British advance from Sword Beach. A few German tanks

Convinced that the weather was too severe for the Allies to attempt a landing, Major General Edgar Feuchtinger, commander of the 21st Panzer Division (below), was in Paris on the night of 5 June.

IT'S UP TO

US TO LET 'EM HAVE IT!

did in fact reach the coast in the gap between Sword Beach and Juno Beach, but not in sufficient numbers to cause serious disruption. By the end of the day, the 21st Panzer Division had lost a quarter of its armored strength yet was still deployed to bar the Allies' way into Caen.

By evening on D-Day, the Allies had managed to land 130,000 men on the beaches, plus another 22,000 dropped by air. The entire assault force had suffered only 8600 casualties. This was in itself an incredible achievement, but few of the immediate D-Day objectives had actually been met. The British 3rd Division had failed to take Caen, and the Canadians had been unable to capture the airfield at Carpiquet. The American troops landed on Utah had pushed several miles inland to link up with the airborne divisions, but the situation at Omaha, where the bridgehead was in places still less than half a mile deep, gave rise to great concern. Before any attempt could be made to capture Cherbourg, the two American bridgeheads had to be united into a solid front and the road junction and bridges at the town of Carentan had to be captured.

Carpiquet airfield (above), a couple of miles to the west of Caen, remained firmly in German hands on the evening of D-Day. Stiff resistance from a German infantry division had stopped the Canadians well short of their objective. It took weeks of bitter fighting before the Allies were able to capture its cratered ruins.

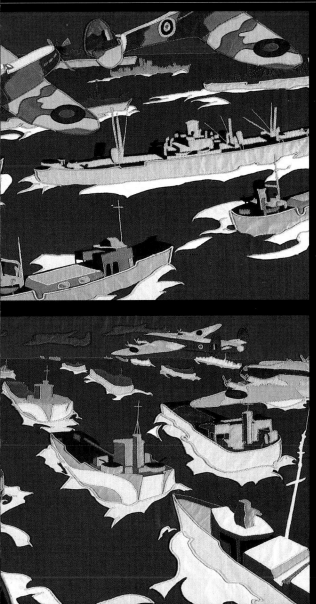

The Overlord Embroidery

Conceived as a modern counterpart to the 11th-century Bayeux tapestry, which commemorates the Norman invasion of England in 1066, this "patchwork" was pieced together by students at London's Royal School of Needlework between 1968 and 1973. The embroidery, comprised of thirty-four panels together measuring 272 feet long, is kept at the D-Day Museum in Portsmouth, England. Pieces of fabric from actual battle uniforms lend poignancy and authenticity to the work. Here and on the following pages are a few scenes from this remarkable tribute to the people who so bravely fought for the principles of liberty and democracy.

Despite the fact that several of its planned objectives had not been met, the naval phase of Overlord, Operation Neptune, was deemed a success—certainly it claimed far fewer casualties than had been anticipated. The next step for the Allies was to accumulate sufficient forces in Normandy to defeat the German divisions there and then to head east toward the Seine.

CHAPTER IV
CONSOLIDATION

Troops from the US 29th Infantry Division move into the battered ruins of Saint-Lô on 18 July (opposite).

German panzer division commanders Kurt Meyer, Fritz Witt, and Max Wunsche (left to right).

This stage of the campaign was essentially a race between the two sides. Montgomery knew he had to seize sufficient territory to form a base of operations, while simultaneously bringing fresh divisions ashore and stockpiling the supplies, ammunition, vehicles, and fuel required for the trek across France. If he could do so more quickly than the Germans could bring in their own reinforcements, he would win the battle.

Air superiority was critical, and, fortunately, by D+1 (the day following D-Day—or 7 June —according to the military calendar) American and British fighter-bombers were able to operate from improvised airstrips in Normandy, which considerably extended the amount of time they could spend in the air. The fighter-bombers' ability to hinder the movement of German reinforcements was one of the key factors in the eventual victory.

SMA

The one factor over which Montgomery had no control was the weather, which continued to severely delay all incoming shipments of troops and supplies. Until Cherbourg could be captured and its port facilities made operational, everything had to be either landed on the open beaches or transported through the two mulberry harbors.

Montgomery's small tactical headquarters had left England for Normandy on 6 June. He himself embarked on a destroyer that evening. The following morning, he cruised along the beaches and conferred with General Bradley, who—aboard the USS *Augusta*—was similarly occupied. Montgomery instructed Bradley to concentrate first on joining the two American beachheads, Utah and Omaha, across the Vire River estuary. At the same time he ordered Lieutenant General Miles C. Dempsey, commander of the British Second

SHING AHEAD!

Nazis Say We're 10 Miles In;

Army forces, to surround Caen by advancing simultaneously to the east and west of the city. Bayeux, to the northwest, had been captured early on D+1, and British forces now controlled the main road between the two cities, but Dempsey was in dire need of reinforcements and supplies before he could complete his mission.

The Enemy's Reaction

Thanks to the convincing work of Allied double agents and the overwhelming success of Fortitude, the German high command still resolutely believed that the landings in Normandy were a feint for a more major landing still to come. Hitler refused to allow the relocation of any of the units stationed north of the Seine. To fend off Dempsey's

British troops marching into Bayeux on 7 June (opposite above).

Montgomery and his army commanders in Normandy (left). On his left is General Miles Dempsey. On his right is General Omar Bradley.

One of the young soldiers of the 12th SS Panzer Division, the "Hitler Jugend" (above).

forces, Rommel therefore had to make do with his own reserves and consequently ordered one of his panzer divisions in southern France to move north.

But the opportunity for Rommel to stage a heavy armored counterattack had passed. By the time the division arrived, the British were well dug in. The only other panzer division within striking distance mistakenly attempted to move in broad daylight and suffered heavy losses from Allied fighter-bombers. The movement of German infantry reserves from Brittany was equally hampered by lack of fuel and chaotic conditions on the railway system.

The Allied Front

With the capture of the small harbor of Port-en-Bessin, the British were finally able to join the Americans in an

expansion of the Omaha bridgehead. The US V Corps had made an astonishing recovery from their disastrous landing on Omaha, and on the morning of 9 June Montgomery was able to order Bradley to move this corps southward toward Coutances and Saint-Lô—both inland towns located at the base of Cotentin Peninsula—to cover Dempsey's western flank. Within two days, the Allies had enlarged the area under their control to a depth of more than twelve miles.

At the same time, the US 101st Airborne was fighting its way toward Carentan, and on the evening of 11 June

An American Thunderbolt fighter-bomber (left). Such aircraft were greatly feared by the Germans. Armed with bombs and rockets, they could fly over the battlefield and sweep down on unprotected enemy formations, forcing the Germans to move their troops only by night.

As German resistance around Caen stiffened, the city's capture proved to be more and more difficult. British troops found themselves fighting for the ruins of Normandy villages, the stone houses of which were easily turned into strongholds by the enemy.

On 14 June General Charles de Gaulle was finally permitted to set foot in liberated France. Escorted by military police (below), he went to Bayeux, where he made a speech. After a brief meeting with Montgomery, the general was returned to the beach at Courseulles and embarked for England, to the great relief of the Allied political and military leaders.

the last defenders there surrendered, enabling the two American groups to unite in a cohesive front at last. From Carentan, Bradley's men were to head slightly south to cut off the peninsula and then north to capture Cherbourg. The British and Canadians would assist by detaining as many units of the German armored divisions as possible in the vicinity of Caen.

Fighting in the *Bocage*

The Allies had sixteen divisions ashore by 11 June, facing elements of fourteen German ones, but fifteen thousand men had been lost, and delivery of supplies was still twenty-four hours behind schedule. Dempsey's army, blocked by a panzer division about ten miles west of Caen, at Tilly-sur-Seulles, was already exhausted. To make matters worse, the soldiers found themselves in territory known as *bocage,* countryside dense with tall

hedgerows lining ancient sunken roads with steep, stony sides—perfect for defensive maneuvering. Tanks were rendered useless because of the deep gullies, and the only way forward was for infantry troops to blast a passage through, field by field, stone farmhouse by stone farmhouse.

Montgomery's frustration was further fueled by British Air Chief Marshal Leigh-Mallory's refusal to provide aircraft for a proposed airborne landing in the highly unsuitable terrain. In fact, by 13 June, a temporary stalemate had descended upon the battlefield, and Montgomery had to call a halt to his plans, both for the envelopment of Caen and for the American breakout into Brittany via Saint-Lô. The enemy had managed temporarily to recapture Carentan, and the British 7th

Armored Division, the famous "Desert Rats," were unable to claim Villers-Bocage, a small town south of Bayeux.

The good news was that the Allies' widespread efforts had succeeded in forcing Rommel to commit his armor piecemeal and use it defensively. They had prevented him from consolidating his tanks and mounting a massive counterstroke.

Above: An aerial view of the mulberry harbor at the eastern end of Omaha Beach. In the foreground is the end of the outer wall of caissons that form the breakwater. Inside are anchored merchant ships and landing craft. Three of the floating pierheads were joined to the shore by floating roadways (left), which were strong enough to carry tanks and columns of trucks.

Logistical Problems Impeded the Allies

The first components of the mulberries had arrived in Normandy on D+1, and by 18 June most of the outer caissons for the two harbors were in position and installation of the floating pierheads was underway. In

By 18 June, the two mulberry harbors were in position and fully operational. But then disaster struck, in the form of a ferocious storm. The outer lines of massive concrete caissons were breached by the waves, wreaking havoc inside (left below). The floating roadways were torn apart and flung up onto the beaches. Ships broke their moorings and sank, adding to the confusion. Although the harbor at Arromanches was able to be repaired, the one at Omaha was abandoned, thus further delaying the buildup of supplies.

the early hours of 19 June, however, a vicious storm swept up the Channel and sank several sections of the floating roadway that was being towed across. The tempest, which raged for three whole days, completely demolished the American mulberry at Omaha Beach and severely damaged the British one at Gold Beach. Hundreds of landing craft were stranded on the beaches or sank

YANKS CH

offshore, and unloading came virtually to a standstill. Montgomery's plan to attack across the Odon River (a tributary of the Orne) at Caen to keep up the pressure on Rommel in that area had to be abandoned, unavoidably giving the enemy a chance to rest and regroup.

The Cherbourg Campaign

Meanwhile, in the west of the peninsula, Major General Joseph Lawton Collins and the US VII Corps brilliantly exploited the situation created by the lack of enemy strength in the region. One of the US Army's "bright young men" and one of the best fighting generals of the war, "Lightning Joe" Collins pushed his GIs through the thinly manned German line in a series of short stabbing moves. Early on the morning of D+12 (18 June), his advance units marched into the tiny seaside village of Barneville-Carteret, on the

Left: "Lightning Joe" Collins, the charismatic commander of the US VII Corps.

RGE AT HEART OF CHERBOURG

Opposite above: A German Panzer Mark IV tank moving up to the front.

Cherbourg was the only port in Normandy capable of berthing oceangoing ships, hence the importance of its capture to the Allied buildup in Europe. Well fortified by the Germans, on land it could be approached only via narrow gorges in the surrounding hills. Once the Americans had taken the hillcrests above the town on 24 June (left above), the fate of Cherbourg was sealed. General von Schlieben (left below) and his staff soon surrendered.

west coast of Cotentin Peninsula, opposite Utah Beach. The entire peninsula was thus effectively cut off by the Americans, and the remaining German forces there were for all intents and purposes surrounded.

Giving the enemy no chance to react, Collins had three divisions ready to move north the following morning. Forgoing a preliminary artillery bombardment, the US 4th Infantry Division surprised the enemy in Montebourg, on the southeastern coast of the peninsula. Moving rapidly, by the evening of 24 June the Americans had reached the heights overlooking Cherbourg.

German defense of this strategic port should have been strong, but the garrison commander, General Karl-Wilhelm von Schlieben, lacked the manpower to take full advantage of the concrete bunkers and trenches. In all he had twenty-one thousand men, but many of them were naval personnel, construction workers, and foreign "volunteers"—not trained soldiers.

Collins concentrated his three divisions on the port, using reconnaissance units to watch his flanks, and made extensive use of naval artillery and fighter-bombers to pin down the defenders. His infantry units then crept forward and blasted the enemy from bunker to bunker. In vain, von Schlieben issued old French rifles to cooks and supplymen, obeying Hitler's order that the harbor and city had to be defended to the last man.

By the evening of 26 June, the Americans had entered Cherbourg and captured von Schlieben, who is said to have commented wryly to his captors, "You cannot expect Russians and Poles to fight for Germany against Americans in France." The American flag was hoisted triumphantly atop Fort du Roule, an ancient stronghold on the hills above the city. Sadly, it was soon discovered that enemy demolition engineers had done a thorough job on Cherbourg's port installations, and it was several weeks before it could be reopened for Allied use.

Operation Epsom: The Battle of the Odon

The fall of Cherbourg permitted Bradley to move his troops east toward Saint-Lô at the end of the month. Unfortunately, this phase of the operation placed the Americans in the middle of the deadly *bocage,* where they were to be faced with severe losses until they could gain adequate footing for a breakout. While Bradley regrouped and accumulated stores of ammunition, Montgomery plotted a move across the Odon to the west

General Richard O'Connor, commander of the British VIII Corps in Normandy (left).

The German "Enigma" coding machine. Rotating drums behind a regular keyboard mechanically scrambled the typewritten messages.

of Caen, in the hopes of keeping Rommel's panzer divisions off balance and away from the Americans.

Although Hitler and his entourage, lulled by Allied deception and the incompetence of their own intelligence services, still maintained that the Allies planned to make another landing in the Pas-de-Calais region, Rommel was reluctantly given a few reinforcements, and by the end of June he had eight panzer divisions in Normandy, two of which had been stripped from the eastern front. (However, there were still more divisions guarding the coast north of the Seine than there were fighting the Allies in the bridgehead.) Rommel's overall aim was to concentrate his armor and, by attacking in the area of Bayeux, separate the British from the Americans and, with any luck, force them to repeat the disaster of Dunkirk.

Montgomery's scheme had been to draw the enemy's attention away from Cherbourg by forcing them to do battle at Caen. Its purpose was more than diversionary, however, as Caen's capture— in conjunction with that of Cherbourg—would ideally position the Allies for the

The ruins of a church in a Normandy village destroyed during Operation Epsom. Epsom was the first major battle between armored units in Normandy, yet it was also a classic infantry battle: Men on foot had to dislodge the enemy from stone houses and advance across open corn fields. In spite of massive artillery support, the British were unable to mount a decisive breakthrough.

breakout toward the Seine. But the unforseen and unrelenting bad weather had caused him a temporary loss of initiative and given his adversary the chance to build up his defenses. Through Allied "Ultra" intelligence (the decoding of German messages sent in military cipher), Montgomery was fully aware of the moves of panzer reinforcements into the battle area, but he was unable to attack until the weather had cleared and his own reinforcements had landed.

For Operation Epsom, Montgomery planned to use two infantry and one armored division on a front only four miles wide, backed by a lethal combination of heavy artillery and tactical air power. The strike was initially scheduled for 21 June, but the stormy seas delayed the landing of supplies, and the target date of the operation had to be postponed for three days.

The temporary lull gave the Germans enough time to establish a strong line of defense comprised of the 12th SS Panzer and units from the 21st Panzer to the east and Panzer Lehr to the west. These were established along the banks of the Orne, which runs through the city's center.

The day the British attack was finally due to begin, the weather was so bad that the fighter-bombers were grounded. But there could be no further delays. Thus, an infantry division, the Scottish 15th, was compelled to lead the way, and the troops quickly became embroiled in hand-to-hand combat among the stone houses along the river. The dismal day ended in a sea of mud and pouring rain.

During the night, the enemy gathered armored reinforcements for a counterattack, but they were unsuccessful. Within a few hours the British infantry had

M any of the troops in the 12th SS Panzer Division—led by Kurt "Panzer" Meyer (left)— were less than eighteen years old, but they proved to be formidable opponents. Their record was marred by the shooting of Canadian prisoners, for which Meyer was sentenced to death in Canada after the war. Reprieved, he served only five years before being released.

General Friedrich Dollmann, the commander of the German Seventh Army (above), was the senior German officer responsible for the defense of Normandy and Brittany. Caught up in Germany's tangled chain of command, he was unable to exert any decisive influence on the battle on D-Day. Later, demoralized by the fall of Cherbourg, he committed suicide.

German tanks camouflaged with branches avoid observation from the air (left). In the German army, only the elite panzer divisions were motorized. The infantry marched, and the bulk of their transport and artillery was horse-drawn.

managed to establish a tenuous bridgehead on the east bank of the Orne.

By 28 June—a day on which both Rommel and von Rundstedt happened to be absent, having been ordered to meet Hitler at Berchtesgaden—Allied tanks were heading toward the captured crossings over the Orne. (It was on this visit to Berchtesgaden that von Rundstedt —having failed to thwart the invasion—was replaced by Field Marshal von Kluge as Supreme Commander in the West.) The most senior German commander in the area, General Friedrich Dollmann, ordered the newly arrived II SS Panzer Corps to mount an immediate counterattack and then—rather than face court-martialling for his role in the loss of Cherbourg—committed suicide.

American soldiers being welcomed by French farmers near Saint-Lô (left).

A Frenchman reading the latest news in one of the Vichy-controlled newspapers (below). Other French citizens preferred to learn about the events of the war from American or British radio.

The Next Day, 29 June, Was a Day of Confusion for Both Sides

The British 11th Armored Division at first managed to capture "Hill 112," an area of high ground south of Caen between the Odon and the Orne, but soon two divisions of the II SS Panzer Corps attacked from the west. Although the British inflicted a crushing defeat on the Germans, Dempsey was convinced that the enemy was planning another, even heavier attack. Worried about the vulnerability of his bridgehead, he ill-advisedly pulled his 11th Armored Division back across the Odon.

This removal of armor enabled the Germans to retake Hill 112, and the fighting rapidly degenerated into small vicious actions reminiscent of trench warfare during World War I. Concerned about the mounting losses, especially among the infantry, Montgomery terminated Operation Epsom on 30 June. According to the VIII Corps war diary, the three divisions involved had suffered more than four thousand casualties—killed, wounded, or missing—during the five-day battle.

Meanwhile, Montgomery had two complete corps—one British and one Canadian—ready to land at Normandy, but the failure to expand the bridgehead meant that he had nowhere to put them. The entire area to the rear of the Second Army was simply choked with supplies and vehicles, with more piling up daily on the beaches as the weather at last began to improve.

The Americans in the *Bocage*

While the British and Canadians were forced into an awkward defensive position, Bradley prepared for his delayed offensive. This plan

A US infantry platoon on 12 July, moving along a typical small road in *bocage* country. The thick hedgerows, many of them centuries old, formed perfect defensive positions and were solid enough to stop tanks. It took a month of bitter fighting before the Americans could establish themselves in a position to break out.

Left: A British soldier hiding in the ruins of a house near Caen.

entailed a broad advance of the entire US First Army to capture the Périers–Saint-Lô road—a span of roughly fourteen miles—in preparation for the breakout into Brittany. On paper, the Americans had a distinct advantage, with four army corps ranged against only six German divisions—several of which were little more than regimental-strength battle groups—along a forty-three-mile front. But the terrain was distinctly unfavorable. There were few roads leading to the east, and the enemy remained in firm control of Saint-Lô

itself, which was the hub of the entire highway network in the area. Several flooded and marshy river valleys lay in the line of advance, and German troops were well positioned on the high ground to the west, around the town of La Haye-du-Puits.

Bradley's offensive got underway on 3 July, with the US VIII Corps—already established on firm ground across the marshy Douve River in the peninsula's center—sending four divisions westward to attack in the direction of La Haye-du-Puits. But, once again, an Allied offensive backed by massive firepower from artillery and aircraft was hindered by stubborn German defense from hedgerow to hedgerow. Although the German troops suffered appalling casualty rates, their morale appeared not to falter as they obeyed their Führer's order to defend every last square foot of ground. Although the Americans

In any war, the medical workers—tending to both their own and enemy wounded—are often the unsung heroes. Working under barrages of shell fire, the unit doctors set up their aid stations in farmhouses right behind the lines, giving first aid to torn and broken bodies. Those who could be saved were evacuated in trucks to field hospitals and from there sent back to England (above left).

The wreckage of a German aircraft in a hangar at the Carpiquet airfield.

managed to capture the town on 8 July, the enemy still retained possession of the surrounding hills. And by 10 July the entire offensive was stalled.

Caen

While the American GIs struggled through the *bocage* in western Normandy, General Montgomery became increasingly frustrated by the inability of the British and Canadians to make any inroads in the Caen sector to the east. The airfield at Carpiquet, two miles to the west of Caen, was still firmly in the hands of the 12th SS Panzer Division, which was also stubbornly defending all possible routes toward the more open country around Falaise. The British needed to gain control of this area if they were to swing northeastward toward the Seine crossings and Paris.

Desperation leading him to revert to sledgehammer tactics, Montgomery decided to carpet bomb Caen and then attempt a direct assault to capture the bridges over the Orne in the city's center. Late in the evening of 7 July, the heavy aircraft of the Royal Air Force Bomber Command dropped six thousand 500- and 1000-pound bombs on the northern part of Caen, turning that fine old Norman city into a heap of rubble. The inhabitants who had not already fled sought shelter in the magnificent abbeys and in the city's hospital.

Although the sight of the bombers boosted the morale of those in the British I Corps who were due to attack the following morning, the devastation actually hindered their progress into the city.

A massive aerial attack by the Royal Bomber Command reduced the historic center of Caen to a field of rubble. Only the shells of the magnificent medieval abbeys and churches survived. The operation may have freed the actual city, but the enemy was still able to block the British attempts to advance south toward Falaise.

Subsequent examination of the ruins found virtually no evidence of dead Germans or wrecked vehicles, and it has been argued that the city was bombed unnecessarily.

In three days of bitter fighting, the infantry struggled through the piles of rubble and bomb craters, taking heavy losses in the process. Eventually the Germans were forced to recede, but only as far as the south bank of the Orne. Thus, the Bourguébus ridge, the expanse of high ground

Soldiers posing for a propaganda photograph on the outskirts of the city.

between Caen and the Falaise plain to the south, remained firmly in enemy hands. And no real gains had been made in terms of territory in which to deploy the troops in England who were anxiously awaiting their turn.

Controversy and Stalemate

Ever since the war, there has raged fierce controversy about the conduct of the fighting in Normandy. As commander of the ground forces, Montgomery was responsible for the actual conduct of operations. But Eisenhower became increasingly dissatisfied by what he regarded as slow progress. In general, he would have preferred a "broad front" strategy, that is, continuous fighting all along the front, all the time. Montgomery, on the other hand, liked to fight a set battle and to concentrate force where it could achieve maximum gains. There were many at SHAEF who shared Eisenhower's impatience, and toward the end of June there was a movement to have Montgomery replaced by General Alexander. (While Eisenhower might have liked to take personal command in Normandy, this action was precluded by his duties as Supreme Commander.) By the end of June, even the Americans in the field were becoming increasingly critical of British slowness. In July Eisenhower gave Bradley the authority to reorganize the American field forces in a way that would free them from Montgomery's control, but Bradley saw no reason to make this shift yet. By D+30 the situation in

General Eisenhower was a frequent visitor to Normandy. He is seen here (left) with General Bradley. Deeply frustrated by what he perceived as a lack of progress in the campaign, he still was not swayed by staff officers in his own headquarters who began to be openly critical of Montgomery and the British generals.

The ruined towns and villages bore witness to the terrible price the Normans paid for their liberation.

While Montgomery (below) continued to be optimistic, the press was beginning to complain about the lack of any tangible progress. Although they had been severely mauled, the Germans were still capable of mounting a strong defense and showed no signs of collapse.

Normandy had devolved into a stalemate. The British forces were ranged over an uneven front line on either side of Caen, and the Americans were trapped in difficult terrain. The main factor in the Allies' favor was the continued success of Operation Fortitude. Still believing that the "real" invasion in the Pas-de-Calais region was imminent, the German high command refused to release troops from north of the Seine. This made it impossible for Rommel to gather a large enough force to mount a conclusive counterattack.

At the time, Montgomery claimed that everything was still going according to his master plan, but many other high-ranking Allied officers began to express their worry that the troops would be sealed off in Normandy. Eisenhower, recognizing that the Allied forces had inflicted terrible casualties on the enemy, remained confident that it was only a question of time before German resistance would snap. But where?

Montgomery now came under intense political pressure to achieve a victorious end to the campaign in Normandy, yet he found himself constantly hampered by the enemy's remarkably stubborn defensive tactics and the poor weather. Brought dangerously close to a position of stalemate, he had to produce a visible result—quickly.

CHAPTER V

FROM NORMANDY TO PARIS

Patton, Bradley, and Montgomery (left to right) confer just before the breakout that would complete the Allied campaign in Normandy (opposite). The cover of a 1944 issue of the German armed forces magazine *Signal* (right) shows two SS soldiers in Villers-Bocage.

The search for a strategy was the main topic of discussion at a meeting attended by Montgomery, US Army Commander Bradley, and British Army Commander Dempsey on 10 July—a point when the endeavors of both armies were not going exactly to plan. All three men were deeply frustrated by the Allies' seeming inability to punch a hole through the fragile crust of the German defenses and move beyond the difficult terrain.

Montgomery was desperate for the American troops to turn the corner into Brittany and capture ports there. He was also aware that, unless British forces kept up pressure on the German armor stationed around Caen, the Americans might well become stuck in the *bocage*. As a result of this conference, a new directive was issued. With certain modifications, this breakout strategy identified the various movements that eventually led to victory in Normandy.

Operation Cobra

Dempsey was ordered first to clear the Germans out of the southern suburbs of Caen and then to attack over the Orne toward Thury-Harcourt, a town twelve miles to the south. To help him achieve such a breakthrough, three armored divisions were pulled out of line and assembled as a separate corps. (Until then, tanks had had little effect on the fighting in Normandy—they were practically useless in the *bocage*—and the brunt of the losses had been borne by the infantry.) Bradley, meanwhile, was to fight his way eastward and, upon reaching the town of Avranches, push one corps into Brittany and the rest of the army southeast toward Alençon and Le Mans. The two army commanders retired to

It fell to General Dempsey (left) to break the stalemate on the British front by clearing the Germans out of the southern suburbs of Caen. At the same time, he had to engage the attention of the enemy panzer divisions to keep them away from the American front, where Bradley was struggling to move out of the *bocage*.

their headquarters to work out plans for their respective operations, each designed to gain a foothold on more favorable terrain rather than to achieve a great victory.

Bradley studied his maps carefully and decided on a concentrated strike along a narrow front. For this he chose the Périers–Saint-Lô road. His plan, known as Operation Cobra, was to launch a massive air bombardment—using the road, easily visible from the air, as a guide—immediately followed by an all-out attack by the VIII Corps. Two infantry divisions would advance right behind the bombers keeping the shoulders of the gap they created open, while behind them, two armored divisions would charge through.

American troops advancing in the Saint-Lô area (below). On the left, heavily laden infantry march beside the road, while, on the right, a jeep carrying spools of signal wire heads for the front line. In conformance with Montgomery's strategy, it was the Americans who would break out to the south of Cotentin Peninsula while the German armor was engaged against the British around Caen. General Bradley had the troops and equipment to accomplish this, but many of his units were held up by determined German defenders in the *bocage,* and poor weather diminished the effectiveness of Allied air power. What is remarkable about the Normandy campaign is how quickly the relatively inexperienced American units developed into a strong fighting force. Most of the young GIs arrived in France fresh from their training camps.

Units of the British Second Army clearing a German ambush site (left). The area chosen for Operation Goodwood—like Epsom, named after a famous British racetrack —was extremely restricted. Plus, the enemy had excellent observation posts in the eastern suburbs of Caen and on the high ground to the south of the city.

For his part, General Dempsey was not happy about the idea of continuing the futile and costly infantry battles along the Odon and instead came up with what he considered a better solution. His plan, known as Operation Goodwood, was to capture the Bourguébus ridge—an area of high ground that acted as the gateway to the road between Caen and Falaise—using the three armored divisions. Once the enemy was locked in battle there, the rest of the Second Army would activate to the west of Caen, thereby—he hoped—catching the Germans off guard. Goodwood was originally timed to start on 17 July, two days before the launch of Bradley's Operation Cobra, but was postponed for twenty-four hours.

Operation Goodwood

The site near Caen where the British armored divisions would have to assemble was very restricted and could be observed easily by the enemy, massed along the high ground to the south. In addition, the battlefield was crossed by two railway lines running along high embankments. To overcome such topographical disadvantages, Dempsey planned a heavy air bombardment just before the assault by the ground forces. As his comments at the time show, he was optimistic that the German resistance would crumble quickly. He did not know, however, that the Germans were aware that the British were coming, had no intention of giving up, and had built up a series of strong defensive positions well equipped with anti-tank guns. The enemy had a number of heavy Tiger tanks and plenty of the deadly 88-mm guns that could penetrate the more lightly armored Allied tanks. (Ironically, the day before Goodwood was mounted, on 17 July, Rommel was severely wounded when his staff car was strafed by a fighter aircraft. He was replaced by von Kluge and played no further role in the Normandy campaign.)

Early on the morning of 18 July, the Germans found themselves on the receiving end of what was at the time the heaviest air attack on ground troops ever launched. Thousands of tons of bombs rained down, saturating the area around the Bourguébus ridge. The bombing was followed by the massed artillery of three army corps coupled with heavy gunfire from warships out at sea. In theory, none of the enemy should have survived.

However, as the lead units of British General G. P. B. Robert's division stormed toward Bourguébus, they were engaged by a battle group of the 21st Panzer Division in

One of the most successful weapons developed during World War II was the German 88-mm anti-tank gun. The photograph below shows a towable version. Other models of the gun —notably the powerful Koenigstiger (King Tiger) tank destroyer— were mounted on self-propelled chassis. The 88-mm artillery could easily penetrate the armor of the various models of Allied tanks used in the Normandy invasion.

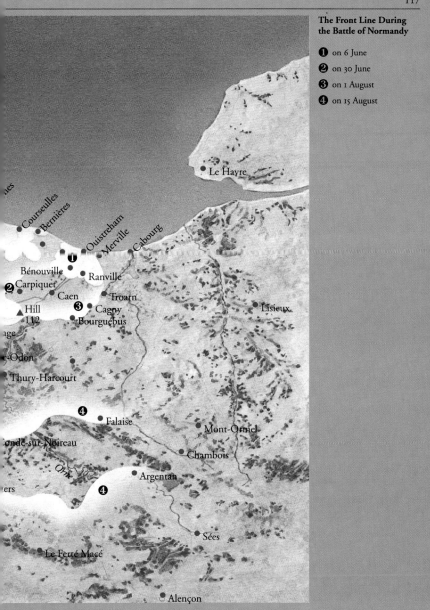

**The Front Line During
the Battle of Normandy**

❶ on 6 June

❷ on 30 June

❸ on 1 August

❹ on 15 August

the village of Cagny. Sixteen British tanks were destroyed immediately, and by midday the advance had shuddered to a halt. The 7th Armored Division had not even crossed the start line. Dempsey began to realize that he had lost the valuable momentum gained by the air attack. Lacking the effects of speed and surprise, the battle soon degenerated into what Dempsey had wished at all costs to avoid—another infantry struggle.

By evening the southern suburbs of Caen had been cleared of the enemy, although the struggle continued for two days before a toehold was gained on the ridge. While on a map the results might seem hardly worth the casualties, the British had finally cleared Caen, and the Odon and Orne were now behind them. In spite of their own losses of men and tanks, they had so irreparably

Two of the V-1 flying bombs that Hitler ordered launched against southern England (above). Although many were intercepted and shot down, sufficient numbers reached their targets, resulting in political pressure for an early capture of their launch sites in northern France.

A jeep from the US 2nd Armored Division on a muddy track in the *bocage* (below).

The "rhinoceros," a modified Sherman tank (above).

Deeply disappointed by the failure of Goodwood, Churchill (below) began to lose faith in Montgomery's abilities.

damaged the Germans that von Kluge even acknowledged in a letter to Hitler that he was losing the battle for Normandy. It was simply a question of time.

The 20th of July Was a Fateful Day

In distant East Prussia, a bomb in a briefcase exploded in a failed attempt on Hitler's life. It reassured the Allies to know that there evidently was sufficient dissension within the ranks of the German army to have warranted an assassination plot. Churchill is reported to have said, "They missed the old bastard—but there's time yet."

This time, the disappointing results of Goodwood nearly cost Montgomery his job; Tedder and other officers at SHAEF conspired to have him sacked. Air force commanders accused him of promising decisive results and then failing to press the ground attack after their bombardment. American staff officers claimed that their men were taking the heaviest losses while the British sat around Caen doing nothing. This was patently untrue, of

course, but the controversy would smolder in the background throughout the rest of the war in Europe.

There was a real reason, however, for the feeling of desperation. Attacks on London and southern England by German V-1s, unmanned flying missiles fired from bases north of the Seine, had begun in mid June and were exacting heavy tolls on British lives and property. The people of England were demanding an end to the menace, and it was easy for them—and their elected representatives—to accuse the armies in Normandy of doing nothing.

Operation Cobra

While the British troops were embroiled in the Goodwood carnage, the Americans were establishing a solid foundation for the breakout from the *bocage*. In this they were greatly aided by a new device developed by a clever young American sergeant: To the front of a Sherman tank he welded two sharp steel prongs. As the tank advanced, the prongs bored into the steep sides of the roads, allowing the tank to push through instead of toppling over. (In an ironic twist that especially pleased the soldiers, the scrap metal used to make the prongs came from the obstacles that had been littered across the beaches by the Germans to hamper the Allied landing.)

American engineers quickly assembled several of these improvised bulldozers, nicknamed rhinoceroses.

On the night of 18 July, American forces finally took possession of the ruined remains of Saint-Lô, although its capture cost them nearly ten thousand casualties. The same night, three infantry divisions, backed by two armored divisions, fought their way through to the high ground overlooking the Périers–Saint-Lô road. Facing the Americans were thirty thousand Germans from the Seventh Army and, right in the path of the intended attack, the Panzer Lehr Division, with its tanks well dug in.

In 1943 Patton (above), the legendary commander of the US Third Army, had nearly destroyed his career by striking a soldier he accused of malingering in a field hospital in Italy.

Les troupes allemandes contre-attaquent au sud d'Avranches

GIs from the US 8th Infantry Division, smiles of victory already upon their faces, marching through the ruins of a village on their way to Avranches (left). Operation Cobra finally broke the thin crust of German resistance, making possible the transition from static to mobile warfare.

As far as Bradley was concerned, everything depended on fine weather to give the bombers a clear run to the target. The rain persisted, however, and Cobra was postponed a few more days. Tragically, news of a second delay—this one for twenty-four hours—reached the Allied bombing forces too late, and several hundred tons of bombs were dropped unwittingly on the waiting troops, killing many.

Cobra finally started on the morning of 25 July. For the Germans, the bombing was a frightful experience. The Panzer Lehr Division in particular was severely damaged. As usual, the enemy put up a spirited resistance, and on the first day the Americans were unable to advance even two miles. But the Germans' defenses were sadly depleted, and the American fighter-bombers successfully impeded efforts to gather reinforcements.

The second day of Cobra was indecisive and left Bradley feeling distinctly pessimistic about his chances of achieving a useful result. But, in a turn of events that caught all concerned by surprise, on 27 July an armored division led by Collins suddenly found itself no longer facing any serious opposition.

General Courtney H. Hodges (above), commander of the US First Army after 1 August.

The long-desired goal of mobile warfare had been achieved. A decisive breakout was now possible.

At the Ready Was the Impetuous General Patton, Whose Third Army Became Operational on 1 August

Patton's presence in Normandy was in fact a well-guarded secret. As far as the Germans knew, he was still commanding the fictitious US 1st Army Group in Kent. Considered by many to be something of a martinet (his trademark was a pair of ivory-handled pistols), Patton was a cavalryman with a strong will to leave his mark on history. Now Bradley put him in temporary charge of the US VIII Corps and let him loose to command the armored pursuit of German forces that had unexpectedly been made possible. His mission was to lead the Third Army out of Normandy into the heart of Brittany.

A drawing of one of the rare night raids carried out by the German air force during the battle for Normandy (left).

On 30 July Patton's lead tanks, the 4th Armored Division, drove southward into Avranches and seized that pivotal coastal town. They then quickly swung south to Pontaubault, where a crucial bridge over the Sélune River was captured intact. Next, Patton ordered his VIII Corps to drive on into Brittany. There their progress was virtually unhindered, Hitler having denuded the region of troops to prop up the front in Normandy and the coast of the Pas-de-Calais region. An impressive seven divisions were pushed through Avranches in seventy-two hours, with senior officers standing beside the road directing the traffic.

TYPHOONS & TIGERS IN THE FALAISE GAP

Reconstruction of a scene from the fight to close the Falaise "pocket" (left).

Restructuring the Allied Command

Effective 1 August were a number of major changes at the top of the Allied command structure. The need for such a reorganization of the hierarchy at this stage of the campaign had been anticipated several months earlier by Overlord's planners, and its execution took no one by surprise. Patton's Third Army officially became operative, and Bradley was advanced to command what then became the US 12th Army Group. Command of the US First Army was given to General Courtney H. Hodges. Montgomery's 21st Army Group now consisted of the British Second and Canadian First armies, the latter having been brought in in July. Montgomery maintained overall control of the ground forces for the duration of Overlord, but beginning 1 August he was equal in status to Bradley. From this point on, the enormous preponderance of American troops and equipment increasingly relegated British forces to a secondary role.

By the evening of 1 August, Patton's 4th Armored Division was in the suburbs of Rennes, halfway to the Loire River, and his 6th Armored was heading for Saint-Malo, on the coast. So swift were these advances that it soon became obvious that much of the liberation of Brittany could be left to the French Resistance forces, leaving the Third Army free to turn east. Accordingly, Patton was ordered to head the bulk of his forces toward Le Mans and then on to Orléans, south of Paris, as part of the plan to pin the German forces against the Seine.

Soldiers encountering an enemy tank in a Normandy village (below).

Meanwhile, Plans for a Massive Counterattack Were Being Discussed by Hitler and His Entourage

On 2 August Hitler ordered von Kluge to detach all available armored units, assemble them into a strike force to be directed between Mortain and Avranches, and cut off the Americans in Brittany. He was promised the support of one thousand fighter aircraft. Von Kluge's armored units, however, were still inextricably entangled with the British and Canadians around Caen. By the evening of 6 August, he had succeeded in disengaging only four divisions and Patton's men were already nearly at Le Mans.

Suddenly, during the night of 6 August, the Germans attacked the American infantry division at Mortain. Though the attack was a complete surprise, its thrust soon was blunted by a battalion of American GIs. When dawn broke the following morning the skies were clear and the Allied fighter-bombers were easily able to frighten off any further attempts at penetration by the enemy. Several more days of battle followed, but Bradley—recognizing what von Kluge was attempting to do—quickly saw that he had been handed a golden opportunity.

On 8 August he outlined a new plan to abandon the

Field Marshal Gunther von Kluge, the German Supreme Commander in the West (below), knew full well that the battle for Normandy was lost, but, because of Hitler's orders

to defend every square foot to the end, he was obliged to watch the destruction of his remaining panzer units.

General Philippe de Hautecloque (right), better known as Leclerc, was given command of the French 2nd Armored Division, which landed on Utah Beach on 30 July. Leclerc's division was attached to Patton's XV Corps and took part in the final stages of the closure of the Falaise pocket.

A scene from the battle of Falaise (left).

wide sweep toward the Seine, replacing it with a maneuver that would trap the remainder of the German forces between the Canadians, who were moving south toward Falaise, and Patton's XV Corps, who would be redirected north toward Argentan. Montgomery enthusiastically concurred, and a general mood of euphoria was soon evident among the Allied commanders.

The Falaise "Pocket"

By attempting a counterattack and, even after it had clearly failed, insisting upon its continuation, Hitler had effectively signed the death warrant of the Seventh Army and the armored units in Normandy. While the Germans unwittingly moved their tanks westward into the trap, Patton's armor was heading east toward the Loire at full speed, encountering only odd pockets of resistance.

The withdrawal of the German armor from the area near Bourguébus on the night of 7 August was the cue for the Canadians to mount their southward attack. Although opposed only by infantry and a small reserve formed from the remnants of the 12th SS Panzer, the Canadian II Corps still faced the full weight of German heavy artillery and anti-tank guns. The Canadian corps

commander decided to attack without a preliminary bombardment—and at night. His concentrated armor and infantry would thrust across a narrow front while aircraft simultaneously bombed the flanks to keep the enemy at bay.

Shortly after midnight, a thousand armored vehicles set off southward from Caen. Before the early morning mist forced a delay, they had penetrated nearly three miles through the first two lines of defense. Unfortunately, several of the Canadian units and a Polish armored division were inexperienced and wasted time dealing with isolated enemy strongholds, and, as a result, valuable momentum was lost. The Germans used the opportunity to reorganize. (In this they were capably led by General Kurt "Panzer" Meyer,

French soldiers landing on Utah Beach to assist in the liberation of their country (below).

LANDING IN S. FRANCE

"The Operation Is Going On Extremely Well"

commander of an SS panzer division, who reputedly threatened stragglers back into line at pistol point.)

That same morning, Bradley directed Patton and his forces to attack northward toward Argentan. Von Kluge saw the danger he was in but—aware as he was of the price of disobedience—could do nothing about it. On 12 August the Americans claimed Alençon and by the following evening were in the vicinity of Argentan. A week later, on 19 August, the Polish tanks met the US 90th Infantry at Chambois, five miles northeast of Argentan. The pocket was finally sealed off.

In the final battle, more than ten thousand Germans were killed and an additional fifty thousand taken prisoner. It is estimated that twenty thousand managed to escape. Over the battlefield hung the stench of dead men, horses, and cattle, and the lanes were choked with the wreckage of tanks, trucks, and guns—the remains of nineteen of the enemy's divisions.

Success!

To the northeast, Patton's Third Army relentlessly pursued the retreating Germans across France to the Seine. Three days later, the American, British, and Canadian armies were aligned along the river northwest of Paris.

The Allied leaders had every reason to rejoice. Their skillful, often brilliant manipulation of staggeringly large numbers of Allied naval, air, and ground elements had been rewarded with a decisive victory. The Normandy campaign had drawn to a successful conclusion, and the longed-for vanquishing of Hitler and the Nazi war machine was in sight.

The closure of the Falaise pocket opened to the Allies the long straight roads that lead to Paris (above).

Allied troops disembarking from a landing craft on the Côte d'Azur, in southern France (opposite).

An American GI guards young German prisoners of war.

DOCUMENTS

"Real war is never like paper war,
nor do accounts of it read
much the way it looks."

—Ernest Hemingway

A Leader for Overlord

In 1946, scarcely a year after the end of the war, General Omar N. Bradley undertook to write his account of the American campaign in Europe. In this memoir, A Soldier's Story *(published in 1951), Bradley writes that he was trying "to explain how war is waged on the field from the field command post. For it is there, midway between the conference table and the foxhole, that strategy is translated into battlefield tactics."*

Here, General Bradley explains how the members of SHAEF were chosen.

The selection of a Supreme Commander for OVERLORD had been under advisement as long ago as January, 1943, during the ANFA conference [so-named because it was held at the Anfa Hotel] at Casablanca. At that time, when the cross-channel invasion was being planned for 1943, it was anticipated that the assault would be primarily British. For that reason the conferees proposed that Britain name the Supreme Commander.

When the OVERLORD invasion was later postponed to 1944, British predominance in the assault gave way to the massive manpower reserves of the United States. Churchill stuck by his Casablanca declaration and recommended that now an American be named Supreme Commander. At Quebec the Prime Minister suggested to President Roosevelt that General Marshall be the man. If ever a man deserved the appointment, that man was General Marshall. Yet in the army hierarchy of command the appointment of General Marshall as Supreme Commander would have entailed a stepdown from his post as Army Chief of Staff. But stepdown or no, had General Marshall left Washington to go to Europe, no one—not even Eisenhower—could have taken his place.

In the army we often scoff at the myth of the indispensable man, for we have always maintained that Arlington Cemetery is filled with indispensable men. General Marshall, however, was an exception, for if ever a man was indispensable in a time of national crisis, he was that man.

General Omar N. Bradley.

Roosevelt and Churchill, among others, at the Quebec conference in August 1943.

In the end it was Roosevelt who made the decision to keep Marshall at home.... With General Marshall out of the running, the next logical choice for Supreme Commander fell upon the incumbent of a comparable post in the Mediterranean Theater. For after having defeated the Axis in Tunisia and Sicily, Eisenhower was now forcing his way up the Italian peninsula in that agonizing winter campaign. In terms of experience, tact, and perspective, Ike was admirably equipped for the job. Although some American subordinates thought him too ready a compromiser, especially in Anglo-American disputes, Eisenhower had demonstrated in the Mediterranean war that compromise is essential to amity in an Allied struggle.

I confess that at times I thought Eisenhower too eager to appease the British command, but I admit to having been a prejudiced judge. For as the American field commander I more often than not participated as the Yankee partisan in those disputes.

In early December Eisenhower learned from President Roosevelt that he had been chosen at Cairo to become Supreme Commander for the OVERLORD invasion. With only six months to go before D day, Ike wasted no time in forming the beginnings of a SHAEF staff from among his Mediterranean associates. If ever Eisenhower required an experienced and skillfully trained staff, it would be on the cross-channel invasion.

To serve as deputy commander at SHAEF Eisenhower brought his first-

E isenhower (above) and Montgomery (opposite).

American colleagues in Africa by his modesty, skill, and exemplary discretion as an Allied soldier....

As his chief of staff, Eisenhower named the brilliant, hard-working Bedell Smith, then with him in a similar spot at AFHQ [Allied Force Headquarters] in Caserta. Since England in 1942, the two had become inseparable partners. Although neither had grown excessively dependent upon the other, their relationship had been fused into so much an entity of command that it was difficult to tell where Ike left off and where Bedell Smith began....

To command the British 21st Army Group Eisenhower turned first to his good friend and Tunisian associate, General Alexander. Alexander had accompanied Eisenhower from Tunisia to Sicily to Italy where he commanded the Army Group comprising Clark's and Montgomery's Armies....

Had Alexander commanded the 21st Army Group in Europe, we could probably have avoided the petulance that later was to becloud our relationships with Montgomery. For in contrast to the rigid self-assurance of General Montgomery, Alexander brought to his command the reasonableness, patience, and modesty of a great soldier. In each successive Mediterranean campaign he had won the adulation of his American subordinates.... Although I was unaware of it at the time, the British rejected Eisenhower's bid for Alexander and asked instead that he be retained in Italy to spark the peninsula campaign. Stumped on his request for Alexander, Eisenhower turned to Montgomery....

Psychologically the choice of Montgomery as British commander for the OVERLORD assault came as a stimulant to us all. For the thin, bony, ascetic face

ranking Mediterranean airman to England. A taciturn pipe-smoking Briton, Air Chief Marshal Tedder had earned the trust and affection of his

that stared from an unmilitary turtle-neck sweater had, in little over a year, became a symbol of victory in the eyes of the Allied world. Nothing becomes a general more than success in battle, and Montgomery wore success with such chipper faith in the arms of Britain that he was cherished by a British people wearied of valorous setbacks....

Even Eisenhower with all his engaging ease could never stir American troops to the rapture with which Monty was welcomed by his. Among those men the legend of Montgomery had become an imperishable fact.

Omar N. Bradley
A Soldier's Story, 1951

General Bernard L. Montgomery, commander of the British 21st Army Group, describes his overall ground strategy for Overlord.

My master plan for the land battle in Normandy...was so to stage and conduct operations that we drew the main enemy strength on to the front of the Second British Army on our eastern flank, in order that we might the more easily gain territory in the west and make the ultimate break-out on that flank—using the First American Army for the purpose. If events on the western flank were to proceed rapidly it meant that we must make quick territorial gains there. On the eastern flank, in the Caen sector, the acquisition of ground was not so pressing: the need *there* was by hard fighting to make the enemy commit his reserves, so that the American forces would meet less opposition in their advances to gain the territory which was vital on the west....

Once on shore and firmly established, I began to get this strategy working and

after the heavy battles in the Caen area, and the overrunning of the Cherbourg peninsula, it began to take shape.

Bernard L. Montgomery
The Memoirs of Field Marshal the Viscount Montgomery of Alamein, 1960

Operation Fortitude

Fortitude's primary purpose was to conceal the Allies' strategy for the naval phase of Overlord, Operation Neptune. This was accomplished through a variety of methods—including giving the Germans false information, deceiving them about the date of the landings, and, above all, persuading them that the invasion would take place in the Pas-de-Calais region.

"Garbo," a double agent employed by the Allies to deceive the German high command, played a critical role in the deception effort.

The plan, in broad outline, was to create two army groups, one real (Twenty-first Army Group) and one notional (First United States Army Group or FUSAG). When the Twenty-first Army Group went overseas, FUSAG would be left consisting of the U.S. Third Army (real) and the British Fourth Army (notional). In the final stage, when the U.S. Third Army had gone overseas, on about D+30, FUSAG would be left with only notional formations, these being eventually the Fourteenth U.S. Army and the Fourth British Army. In the early stages before D Day the map for the real order of battle showed the main weight of our forces in the Midlands, the west and the southwest; the false order of battle

The engineers' corps built an illusionary army from rubber and wood. The truck, cannon, and tank pictured here are all fake.

showed the main weight in Scotland, the east and the southeast.

Once the false order of battle was firmly fixed in the German mind and the German files, the deduction on their part that the assault must come in the Pas de Calais area was inevitable, and there is abundant evidence that the Germans did in fact swallow the deception plan hook, line, and sinker. A German map of the British order of battle as on 15 May 1944 which was later captured in Italy showed how completely our imaginary order of battle had been accepted and was largely based on the information supplied by the double-cross agents, especially GARBO and BRUTUS....

On D+3 GARBO, after a conference

In anticipation of the Allied landing, Rommel had pointed stakes ("Rommel's asparagus") planted on beaches and in the fields of Normandy to hinder gliders from landing there.

with all his agents, sent over a full report which he requested might be submitted urgently to the German High Command. In this he set out in concentrated form the order of battle in this country, claimed that seventy-five divisions (instead of about fifty) existed at D Day, pointed out that no FUSAG formation was taking part in the attack, and deduced that the real operation was only a diversionary attack shortly to be followed by an assault in the Pas de Calais area....

On 11 June (D+5) an appreciation was sent by Berlin to Madrid stating that "all reports received in the last week from [GARBO] undertaking have been confirmed without exception and are to be described as especially valuable."

It appears indeed that the Germans believed to the end of the chapter that the Pas de Calais attack was intended and would have been delivered if the Normandy attack had not been more successful than had been expected. Evidence of the movements of German troops entirely supports this view.

J. C. Masterman
The Double-Cross System, 1972

History has proven that the Allied deception plan—as a whole and in every one of its component parts—worked magnificently.

If the Germans could be convinced of the existence of FUSAG, they might then believe that the Normandy invasion was a diversion to lure German forces away from the Pas de Calais, and that as soon as they moved to reinforce Normandy, FUSAG would descend upon the Calais area. Hitler was already predisposed to believe that the Pas de Calais would be the main point of the Allied attack, and he had garrisoned the area with the 15th Army,

the strongest force in the West. It was the directive of the Quicksilver ruse to keep that force in place.

There were other components to Fortitude. The operation codenamed "Ironside" was designed to keep the German 1st Army occupied in the region of Bordeaux during the D-Day period by threats of an invasion along the Biscay coast; and "Vendetta" was calculated to achieve the same result with the German 19th Army in the region of Marseilles. The current phase of "Zeppelin" would continue to put pressure on the Balkans during the D-Day period; and "Diadem" was designed to pin down Hitler's army in Italy through orthodox military operations. Finally, added to all these were scores of smaller operations with exotic code names that would, it was hoped, distract the attention of the German forces from Normandy during the actual invasion....

On paper, Fortitude was a magnificent fiction with which to surprise and confound the enemy. But would its stratagems work in practice? The enemy was clever, resourceful, powerful—and schooled in the dictum of the General Staff's greatest tutor, [military science scholar Carl von] Clausewitz, who wrote: "A great part of the information obtained in war is contradictory, a still greater part is false, and by far the greatest part is somewhat doubtful." Would the Germans remember that dictum, or could the Allied deception agencies convince them that the fictions of Fortitude were both consistent with their own strategical and tactical beliefs and true beyond a shadow of a doubt?

Anthony Cave Brown
Bodyguard of Lies, 1975

Planning and Training

Beginning in 1943, preparations for the invasion of Normandy began in earnest. Many thousands of American soldiers were shipped off to England to assist in Operation Overlord. A few of them had experienced war before—in North Africa, the Middle East, or Italy—but many others were about to face the enemy for the first time.

Letters written by soldiers to their families in the United States provide glimpses of the trainees' day-to-day existence.

25 May 1945

Our first glimpse of England was at the mouth of the Merci River, which we followed to Liverpool. It was dark when we landed and immediately boarded the train which took us to North Devon to a town called Mortehoe, it was near Woolacombe on the Bristol Channel. There we were assigned to the Assault Training Center. You may have heard about the place where the infantry received its training for the invasion.

The 453rd was the first Dukw [dual-drive amphibious truck] company in the ETO [European Theater of Operations] and as a result was considered an oddity. Generals by the score came down to see us train and operate and many of the later plans were based on the result of their observations.

American soldiers drinking beer at an English pub.

The truth about what really happened at Slapton Sands during Exercise Tiger was kept a secret for many years.

North Devon was an ideal place to be. The beach was large and resembled the French Coast to a certain extent. We were located in a Summer Camp which consisted of small cabins. They were like the tourists cabins found in the U.S.

We made many friends among the people there and spent most of our evenings in a small and old "Pub" called the "Fox Hunters' Inn." It was run by a woman whose husband was a Wing Commander in the RAF. She was a grand person and many evenings after ten PM when the familiar "time please" was sounded we adjourned to the parlor to finish our pint of bitters.

While there the company made a fine record for itself and assisted in training troops for the job ahead. We were on the beach from seven AM until after dark every day in all kinds of weather. We often felt the icy waters of the channel when a Dukw would go down or we would have to go in after somebody. It was an experience that was very valuable to our later operations in France.

Charles S. Dedon,
Letter in the collection of the
Mémorial de Caen

This American GI recalls the enforced secrecy surrounding the ill-fated exercise at Slapton Sands.

On April 1, 1944 we entered our first port upon arriving in England. The Harbor Master shouted over a loud bull horn "Welcome Yanks to England." He was on a large tugboat which was used to open the submarine net to let us enter the harbor.

We were given shore leave the next day and as I was walking down a street I felt a tug on my sleeve and saw a little boy about seven years old. He asked the standard question which all the children in England asked every American serviceman…"You got any gum chum?" You could not buy gum in England, and we always carried some. I asked the chap "You got a sister mister?" He said he did, so I told him to go get his older sister and then I would give him a pack of gum.

Two hours later I felt a tug on my sleeve again and here stood the same little kid and he said I brought my sister. I looked at her and she was about nine years old. What I had hoped was his older sister would be at least a teenager.…

Our next port of call was Plymouth, England where we had to unload a huge crane which had turned over onto its side due to the rough Atlantic crossing. It took special equipment and many hours. Because of this we were not able to go out into the English Channel for a practice landing with several other ships in our flotilla. It became a major disaster. Our ships went out without any war-ship escorts even when it was known that there were several German torpedo boats in the area. These boats known as "E" boats were very fast and capable of speeds up to fifty M.P.H. Our top speed of the L.S.T. was fourteen M.P.H. About midnight the Germans located our ships and sank and damaged several others.

We were told of the incident in detail and threatened with a court-martial if we told any of the civilians when on shore leave. That night we lost 946 American soldiers and sailors. [Most other sources give a casualty figure of approximately seven hundred.]…

It seems that our ships were on the wrong radio frequency when told the operation was cancelled, and not to proceed.

with the training exercise.…

In the first week of June, all the Naval ships were "Sealed." This meant no shore leave for any of us. The loading of troops and equipment had begun. From all over England, tanks, trucks, guns and troops converged on the South coastal ports. I think the whole southern coastline of England must [have] sunk down about two feet with all this weight.

My friend and I were sent ashore to pick up the mail and had stopped by the post office to talk with two friendly girls. They said that they did not believe that the Allies would ever invade Europe. The civilian populous could certainly see the massive troop movements, so I often thought later that maybe the girls were pumping us for times and dates to be forwarded to German Intelligence. We did not tell them that our ships were loaded and we were invading the next day.

Joseph P. Doyon,
Letter in the collection of the
Mémorial de Caen

British soldiers practice disembarking into the water with their folding bicycles.

Corporal Bill Bowdidge of the 2nd Battalion, Royal Warwickshire Regiment, recollects one of the more unusual preparatory exercises.

We were stationed at a camp in Sussex and we knew we were going to be among the assault troops on the invasion, but we didn't know where or when that would be. We knew that one of our roles would involve rapid movement because a few weeks before D-Day the whole company, from the commanding officer downwards, was issued with folding bicycles! I didn't think much about it at the time; when you're a junior soldier you just take whatever comes. I don't think anyone thought what are we doing this for?

I mean you're not paid to think, you just do it, accept it. I can't remember anyone saying "What on earth are we going to use these for?"

There was time for us to take our bikes out on the Sussex roads to practise what we called "cycle marches"—riding out in platoons like a pre-war cycle club, all bunched together, three abreast—and new drill movements were devised. The company would fall in in the usual way with the front wheels of our bicycles pointing to the right at an angle of fifteen degrees, the officers in front of their platoons holding their bicycles in the same way and the company commander, with his bicycle, facing the company. He would give the command to come to attention and turn to the right in column of route. To achieve this, we in the ranks would do a smart right turn and at the same time shuffle our bikes backwards and forwards so that they were facing in the right direction.

While this was going on the officers would wheel their bikes to take up position at the head of their platoons and the sergeants went to the rear. The OC would then shout over his shoulder, "D Company, quick march!" and off we would go. After a few paces the order would be, "D Company, prepare to mount," and then, "D Company, mount!" At this we would all swing our legs over and ride on, still trying to keep our dressing to the left. It was great fun.

Of course we had to carry normal marching order, weighing about fifty pounds, on our backs and consequently we all suffered from saddle sores.

Author's interview
Russell Miller
Nothing Less Than Victory, 1993

Ernest Brewer, a British gunner, does not conceal his frustration in this letter to his mother, written just over a week before D-Day.

28 May 1944

Dear Ma,

Well it looks as though I've well and truly had it now. We are all confined to this dump we have moved into; the camp is sealed—so they say. It seems a rotten trick not to tell us beforehand so that we could let you know that it might be our last time at home. I said it seems a rotten trick—rather it is. We are, so far as I can understand, kept here for security reasons, though I myself can't see what we could give away. We don't know anything....
Yours,
Ern
P.S. What's the betting on where we're going and when?

D-Day Museum
Portsmouth, England
Quoted in Russell Miller
Nothing Less Than Victory, 1993

General Eisenhower provides this apt portrayal of the prevailing mood among the participants on the eve of the assault.

All southern England was one vast military camp, crowded with soldiers awaiting final word to go, and piled high with supplies and equipment awaiting transport to the far shore of the Channel.... The southernmost camps where assault troops were assembled were all surrounded by barbed-wire entanglements to prevent any soldier leaving the camp after he had once been briefed as to his part in the attack. The whole mighty host was tense as a coiled spring, and indeed that is exactly what it was—a great human spring, coiled for the moment when its energy should be released and it would vault the English Channel in the greatest amphibious assault ever attempted.

Dwight D. Eisenhower
Crusade in Europe, 1948

Renowned military historian John Keegan was a child in England at the time of the American "invasion."

And then, suddenly, there were the Americans. There had been portents of their coming, in particular the appearance of a US Office of War Information booklet, snapped up by me from a town bookstall, on the Eighth US Army Air Force (USAAF), filled with photographs of the construction of the airfields from which it was to begin its bombing campaign over Europe, and containing a cut-away drawing of the Flying Fortress, for which, through counting the enormous number of machine-guns it mounted, I quickly formed almost as strong a regard as I already had for the Spitfire. There had been outriders, a scattering of officers in the unfamiliar rig of olive jacket and beige trousers—"pinks and greens," as I subsequently learnt veterans nostalgically describe it—whom I used to see walking home on warm sunlit evenings to the lodgings which had been found for them on the outskirts of the town. On one of these, astounding myself by my forwardness and in flagrant violation of family rules, I tried the formula, which I knew to be in universal circulation, "Got any gum, chum?" and was rewarded by an embarrassed halt—my embarrassment was altogether greater—a rummaging in pockets and the presentation of a packet of Spearmint.

As it happened, I did not like chewing gum. But the superiority of the American over the British product, and particularly the sumptuousness of the wrapper and the lustrous simplicity of its design, instantly and deeply impressed me. Much of that evening, which would normally have been spent reading at a gap illicitly opened in my bedroom curtains, I devoted to a study of its elements, struggling in an increasingly trancelike state to draw from its symbolism the message which I sensed the designer sought to convey. Thus I made my first encounter with the science of semeiotics; but also with the bottomless riches of the American economy.

They were shortly to be made manifest in super-abundance. Towards the end of 1943 our backwater, which British soldiers had garrisoned so sparsely for four years, overflowed almost overnight with GIs. How different they looked from our own jumble-sale champions, beautifully clothed in smooth khaki, as fine in cut and quality as a British officer's—an American private, we confided to each other at school, was paid as much as a British captain, major, colonel—and armed with glistening, modern, automatic weapons, Thompson sub-machine-guns, Winchester carbines, Garand self-loading rifles. More striking still were the number, size and elegance of the vehicles in which they paraded about the countryside in stately convoy. The British army's transport was a sad collection of underpowered makeshifts, whose dun paint flaked from their tinpot bodywork. The Americans travelled in magnificent, gleaming, olive-green, pressed-steel, four-wheel-drive juggernauts, decked with what car salesmen would call optional extras of a sort never seen on their domestic equivalents—deep-treaded spare tyres, winches, towing cables, fire-extinguishers.

There were towering GMC six-by-sixes, compact and powerful Dodge four-by-fours and, pilot fishing the rest or buzzing nimbly about the lanes on independent errands like the beach buggies of an era still thirty years ahead, tiny and entrancing jeeps, caparisoned with whiplash aerials and sketchy canvas hoods which drummed with the rhythm of a cowboy's saddlebags rising and falling to the canter of his horse across the prairies. Standing one day at the roadside, dismounted from my bicycle to let one such convoy by, I was assaulted from the back of each truck as it passed by a volley of small missiles, which fell into the ditch beside me.... But when I burrowed in the dead leaves to discover the cause I unearthed…a little treasure of Hershey bars, Chelsea candy and Jack Frost sugar-cubes, a week's, perhaps a month's ration, of sweet things casually disbursed in a few seconds. There was, I reflected as I crammed the spoil into my pockets, something going on in the west of England about which Hitler should be very worried indeed.

John Keegan
Six Armies in Normandy, 1982

The Leaders

The months of secret preparations were over. Paratroopers had been dropped over Normandy, and the assault forces had landed on the beaches. Now was the time for the Allied leaders to proclaim the success of these events— and their plans for the weeks to come—to the citizens of their respective countries.

The Allies

This statement was read to the members of Great Britain's House of Commons by Prime Minister Winston Churchill on 6 June 1944.

I have to announce to the House that during the night and the early hours of this morning the first of the series of landings in force upon the European continent has taken place. In this case the liberating assault fell upon the coast of France. An immense armada of upward of 4000 ships, together with several thousand smaller craft, crossed the Channel. Massed airborne landings have been successfully effected behind the enemy lines, and landings on the beaches are proceeding at various points at the present time. The fire of the shore batteries has been largely quelled. The obstacles that were constructed in the sea have not proved so difficult as was apprehended. The Anglo-American Allies are sustained by about 11,000 first-line aircraft, which can be drawn upon as may be needed for the purposes of the battle. I cannot of course commit myself to any particular details. Reports are coming in in rapid succession. So far the commanders who are engaged report that everything is proceeding according to plan. And what a plan! This vast operation is undoubtedly the most complicated and difficult that has ever taken place. It involves tides, winds, waves, visibility, both from the air and the sea standpoint, and the combined employment of land, air and sea forces in the highest degree of intimacy and in contact with conditions which could not and cannot be fully foreseen.

Prime Minister Churchill in conversation with General Montgomery.

There are already hopes that actual tactical surprise has been attained, and we hope to furnish the enemy with a succession of surprises during the course of the fighting. The battle that has now begun will grow constantly in scale and in intensity for many weeks to come, and I shall not attempt to speculate upon its course. This I may say, however. Complete unity prevails throughout the Allied armies. There is brotherhood in arms between us and our friends of the United States. There is complete confidence in the Supreme Commander, General Eisenhower, and his lieutenants and also in the commander of the expeditionary force, General Montgomery. The ardour and the spirit of the troops, as I saw myself, embarking in these last few days, was splendid to witness. Nothing that equipment, science, or forethought could do has been neglected, and the whole process of opening this great new front will be pursued with the utmost resolution both by the commanders and by the United States and British governments whom they serve.

Hansard, 6 June 1944

A report published in The New York Times *on 7 June 1944 about a press conference with President Roosevelt held the previous day conveyed a message of hope to the American people.*

ROOSEVELT AND CHURCHILL PLEASED BY INVASION GAINS

WASHINGTON, June 6—President Roosevelt told a news conference, held thirteen hours after the initial announcement of the invasion of France, that the operation was proceeding according to schedule. He made this statement in a calm, rather low voice, but with obvious satisfaction that his composure did not entirely hide.

"How do you feel about the progress of the invasion?" a reporter asked.

"It's up to schedule," Mr. Roosevelt replied, then smiled.

This was the summation of all of today's dispatches as they were analyzed by the Constitutional Commander in Chief of the Armed Forces of the United States, who, since being awakened early with news that the invasion had started, had read reports and conferred with top-ranking officers.

Small Losses Are Reported

The President added that, as of noon today, General Eisenhower had reported the loss of only two American destroyers and one LST (landing ship, tank), a heavy type of invasion barge. Losses of our air forces in the same period, Mr. Roosevelt added, were about 1 percent of the airplanes involved. There was no figure on personnel casualties.

Other salient points emphasized by the press conference included the following:

1. Tentative dates for the invasion were set last December at the Teheran conference, slated in May or early this month, according to the weather.

2. General Eisenhower alone decided the actual date and place.

3. Marshal Joseph Stalin has known of the plan since Teheran and has been entirely satisfied with it.

4. A "second front" a year ago would have been impossible because of lack of available men and equipment.

5. The war is not over by any means; this operation is not even over, and this is no time for over-confidence.

The President's press conference, a regularly scheduled one, was attended by

181 reporters, who filled the Executive Office almost to capacity. They found Mr. Roosevelt looking tired around the eyes but smiling. He sat at his desk in shirtsleeves, wearing a dark bow tie. He smoked a cigarette stuck into a yellow amber holder.

Mr. Roosevelt said that relatively few persons in the United States knew the tentative date for the invasion and that very few knew the actual date. He added that the actual date was set only a few days ago, being dependent on weather conditions.

It was largely a question of weather in the English Channel, the President emphasized. Longtime charts indicate that the first good weather each year occurs at this season, and for the invasion small-boat weather was necessary. He confirmed reports that the invasion was postponed for twenty-four hours at the last moment because of adverse weather.

When a reporter asked if the invasion of France was timed to occur after the fall of Rome, the President replied emphatically in the negative, saying that no one knew when Rome would fall.

Roosevelt Hails Invasion Success

The first consideration of this invasion, Mr. Roosevelt went on, began early in 1941 in talks between himself and the Chiefs of Staff, and the plans have been consistently carried forward. Only military men, he emphasized, could understand the vast requirements for the undertaking, not the politicians who a year ago clamored for a second front.

He recalled that before the entry of the United States into the last war a political figure had said that America was always safe, because if this country should be attacked 1,000,000 men

would spring to arms. The problem, Mr. Roosevelt said, was providing the arms.

We had to wait and do what we could, he added, although the plans came gradually to a head, first at the Cairo conference, and afterward at Teheran. The last six months of preparation particularly made a great deal of difference, with the vast additions of men and materiel to the forces overseas.

The President said that the choice of landing places had been made since the Teheran conference. He refused to be drawn into a discussion of possible other attack points or other matters of strictly military information.

Mr. Roosevelt said he had no information as to how much surprise figured in the initial success of the landing operations; he also had no reports on operations by the French underground.

When he was asked to summarize his own personal reaction to the news, he said substantially that the whole country was extremely thrilled but that he hoped it would not develop over-confidence. He told reporters that you just don't land on a beach and walk to Berlin.

As for his hopes, he told a questioner he had only one desire, to win the war and win it 100 percent.

When a reporter told the President that an Axis radio station had broadcast yesterday that the invasion would not occur this month because Mr. Roosevelt planned to go to England late in June the President shrugged and laughed.

The New York Times, 7 June 1944

EISENHOWER'S "ORDER OF THE DAY"

Soldiers, Sailors and Airmen of the Allied Expeditionary Force!

You are about to embark upon the Great Crusade, toward which we have striven these many months. The eyes of the world are upon you. The hopes and prayers of liberty-loving people everywhere march with you. In company with our brave Allies and brothers-in-arms on other Fronts, you will bring about the destruction of the German war machine, the elimination of Nazi tyranny over the oppressed peoples of Europe, and security for ourselves in a free world.

Your task will not be an easy one. Your enemy is well trained, well equipped and battle-hardened. He will fight savagely.

But this is the year 1944! Much has happened since the Nazi triumphs of 1940–41. The United Nations have inflicted upon the Germans great defeats, in open battle, man-to-man. Our air offensive has seriously reduced their strength in the air and their capacity to wage war on the ground. Our Home Fronts have given us an overwhelming superiority in weapons and munitions of war, and placed at our disposal great reserves of trained fighting men. The tide has turned! The free men of the world are marching together to Victory!

I have full confidence in your courage, devotion to duty and skill in battle. We will accept nothing less than full Victory!

Good Luck! And let us all beseech the blessing of Almighty God upon this great and noble undertaking.

Dwight D. Eisenhower

The Germans

Field Marshal Karl Gerd von Rundstedt, Hitler's Commander in Chief in the West, placed little faith in the Führer's scheme for defending against the Allies.

The strength of the defences was absurdly overrated. The "Atlantic Wall" was an illusion; conjured up by propaganda—to deceive the German people as well as the Allies. It used to make me angry to read the stories about its impregnable defences. It was a nonsense to describe it as a "wall," Hitler himself never came to visit it, and see what it really was.

Quoted in Sir Basil Henry Liddell Hart
The Other Side of the Hill, 1951

The following are letters from Field Marshal Erwin Rommel to his wife—one written three weeks before and one a week after the landings.

15 May 1944

Dearest Lu,

The middle of May already and still nothing doing, although a pincer attack seems to have started in Italy, which may well be the prelude for the great events of the spring and summer. I've been away for a couple of days, talking to the officers and men. It's quite amazing what has been achieved in the last few weeks. I'm convinced that the enemy will have a rough time of it when he attacks, and ultimately achieve no success.

14 June 1944

[Dearest Lu,]

Very heavy fighting. The enemy's great superiority in aircraft, naval artillery, men and materiel is beginning to tell. Whether the gravity of the situation is realised up above, and the proper conclusions drawn, seems to me doubtful. Supplies are getting tight everywhere. How are you both? Still no news has arrived.

The Rommel Papers
Edited by Sir Basil Henry Liddell Hart
Translated by Paul Findlay, 1953

D-Day: Reports from the Front Lines

The men who landed in Normandy on 6 June 1944 were well aware that they were participating in an unusual adventure, and all were determined to prove themselves worthy of their mission. Meanwhile, on the German side, confusion and panic swept through the defenders of the Atlantic Wall, and disillusionment crept into the hearts of their leaders.

Airborne Operations

Currently a US Congressman from the state of Florida, in 1944 Sam M. Gibbons was a member of the US 101st Airborne Division.

I was 24 years old—a captain—in the 501st Parachute Infantry, a part of the 101st Airborne Division which, together with the 82nd Airborne Division, landed a total of 12,000 parachutists that night. We were the spearhead of the invasion of Europe. I realize that 12,000 sounds like a large force, but when you consider that we had been told there were 70,000 Germans there, you can see what the situation looked like to us....

For this performance our heads had been shaved—the surgeons insisted we'd be easier to sew up that way—our faces and hands blacked to be less visible. We wore a special jumper's combat uniform and boots. All of our clothing, including the long underwear and socks, had been impregnated with a chemical to protect us from poison gas.

We smelled like inside men from the skunk works. Our unique uniforms were made of a heavy cotton cloth—big pockets and lots of them with snap fasteners for quick opening—the jacket collars were high and right below the neck we carried a switchblade knife in a pocket for emergencies like cutting yourself out of your parachute....

We also wore an equipment harness and ammunition belt with thirty rounds of .45 caliber pistol ammo and about one hundred rounds of .30 caliber rifle ammo, two hand grenades, a .45 caliber pistol, loaded and cocked, a .30 caliber folding stock rifle (carbine), loaded and cocked, a ten-inch blade knife strapped to the leg calf for hand-to-hand combat, a canteen with one quart of water, one spoon and canteen cup used as a cooking utensil, some water purification tablets, a combat first aid kit tied to the camouflage material that covered our steel helmets (special helmet liner required so helmet wouldn't be blown off in jump), special first aid kit containing two shots of morphine, sulphur drugs and compress bandages to stop bleeding. In a leg pocket we carried a British-made anti-tank mine because there were plenty of tanks nearby, a gas mask (I stuck two cans of Schlitz beer in mine), an equipment bag containing a raincoat, a blanket, toothbrush, toilet paper and six meals of emergency K rations—a combination shovel and pick for digging in; maps, flashlight, compass; also an "escape kit" containing a very small compass, small hacksaw blade, a map of France printed on silk and $300 worth of well-used French currency. This kit was enclosed in a waterproof container measuring four inches by six inches by one-quarter inch—everyone was encouraged to hide it in a different place on the body—I carried mine inside my sock, just above boot top on my right leg.

We carried two other items in our equipment. We wore our identification (dog tags) on a light metal chain around our necks, taped together so they didn't click or rattle. And at noontime before the invasion we had received our last surprise: A "cricket." This was a metal device made partially of brass and partially of steel. When you depressed the steel it made a snapping sound or a "crick." And when you released the steel part, it would crick again. This was...to be our primary means of identification between friend and foe during the night assault....

So with all this gear on me (the same for about 12,000 others), I was the third man to step out of plane #42, and dropping 800 feet to start what some have called "The Longest Day."

Sam M. Gibbons
Mémorial de Caen

A merican soldiers disembark from their aircraft behind Utah Beach on 6 June 1944.

Members of the British 6th Airborne Division—including Major John Howard's detachment of gliders—landed to the east of Caen.

War is unpredictable. It is a sad fact but true, that in spite of the best efforts of all concerned, matters in war will frequently go awry from the moment the first shot is fired....

The first task, the securing of the bridges over the Orne and the Caen Canal, was allocated to the [British] 5th Parachute Brigade, landing to the north of Ranville and clearing landing grounds for the Advanced Headquarters and anti-tank guns that would arrive later by glider. For the actual capture of the bridges they had under command a glider force of 180 men from the 2nd Oxfordshire and Buckinghamshire Light Infantry and from 249 Field Company Royal Engineers, commanded by Major John Howard. This force would take the bridges at midnight on 5/6th June by coup-de-main.

Major Howard's plan was to crash-land his glider force beside the bridges and overwhelm the defenders before the shock of their arrival wore off. This plan appeared to suffer a setback some days before the invasion when anti-invasion posts sprouted in the fields around the bridges, but his glider pilots were not a bit disconcerted. They considered they could use the posts to run the glider wings against and slow their landing speed....

Like most other airborne operations that night, Howard's task did not go entirely to plan. Of the 6 gliders, 4 landed on target, close to the canal and river bridges. One landed half a mile away. There were still enough men at Bénouville to do the job and James Wallwork describes the attack: "...The troops, encouraged by Major Howard,

sang and (thank heaven) none was airsick. We were right on time and dead on target, thanks to our tug crew, and we saw the French coast in plenty of time to get set. Five, four, three, two, one, Cheers! Cast off! Up with the nose to reduce speed while turning to Course I. That's when the singing stopped. We came in on the final leg at 90 miles per hour and touched down, crashing through several fences in the process and coming to a final stop half way up the river embankment....

"There was only one casualty on landing. The Bren gunner in No. 2 glider was thrown out and drowned in the pond in our field, about which everyone seemed to have avoided asking daft questions during briefing. Johnnie and I revived in a few minutes and with the aid of a medic I managed to crawl free of the debris...."

Sergeant Roy Howard, heading for the Orne bridge, also had a successful crossing. "We were at 1200 ft and there below us the canal and river lay like silver, instantly recognizable. Orchards and woods lay as darker patches on a dark and foreign soil. "It's all right now, Fred, I can see where we are," I said. I thought it looked so exactly like the sand-table model that I had the strange feeling I had been there before....

"Up with the nose and then the heavy rumble of the main wheels as we touched down a few minutes after midnight close to the river bridge. 'You are in the right place, sir,' I shouted to Lieutenant Fox, who seemed both happy and surprised at the same time. With a drumming and crash of army boots, he and his men disappeared into the night."

Robin Neillands
and Roderick de Normann,
D-Day, 1944: Voices for Normandy
1993

German soldiers in Normandy.

The Enemy Reacts

Thanks to the tremendous success of the deception effort, the Germans were ill prepared to counter the Allied assault. Here, two German commanders—Hans von Luck and Edgar Feuchtinger—recall their reactions to the news of the invasion.

About midnight, I heard the growing roar of aircraft, which passed over us. I wondered whether the attack was destined once again for traffic routes inland or for Germany herself. The machines appeared to be flying very low—because of the weather? I looked out the window and was wide awake; flares were hanging in the sky. At the same moment, my adjutant was on the telephone, "Major, paratroops are dropping. Gliders are landing in our section. I'm trying to make contact with No. II Battalion. I'll come along to you at once."

I gave orders without hesitation, "All units are to be put on alert immediately and the division informed. No. II Battalion is to go into action wherever necessary. Prisoners are to be taken if possible and brought to me."

I then went to the command post with my adjutant. The 5 Company of No. II Battalion, which had gone out with blank cartridges, was not back yet from the night exercise—a dangerous situation. First reports indicated that British paratroops had dropped over Troarn....

We telephoned the company commander, who was in a cellar. "Brandenburg, hold on. The battalion is already attacking and is bound to reach you in a few moments."

"Okay," he replied, "I have the first prisoner here, a British medical officer of the 6th Airborne Division."

"Send him along as soon as the position is clear."

In the meantime, my adjutant telephoned the division. General Feuchtinger and his general-staff officer had not come back yet. We gave the orderly officer, Lieutenant Messmer, a brief situation report and asked him to obtain clearance for us for a concentrated night attack the moment the divisional commander returned.

Hans von Luck
Panzer Commander: The Memoirs of Colonel Hans von Luck, 1989

I first knew that the invasion had begun with a report that parachutists had been dropped near Troarn a little after midnight on 6 June. Since I had been told that I was to make no move until I heard from Rommel's headquarters, I could do nothing immediately but warn my men to be ready. I waited impatiently all that night for some instructions. But not a single order from a higher formation was received by me. Realizing that my armoured division was closest to the scene of operations, I finally decided, at 6:30 in the morning, that I had to take some action. I ordered my tanks to attack the English 6th Airborne Division which had entrenched itself in a bridgehead over the Orne. To me this constituted the most immediate threat to the German position.

Hardly had I made this decision when, at seven o'clock, I received my first intimation that a higher command did still exist. I was told by Army Group B that I was now under command of 7th Army. But I received no further orders as to my role. At nine o'clock I was informed that I would receive orders from 84th Infantry Corps and finally at ten o'clock I was given my first operational instructions. I was ordered to stop the move of my tanks against the Allied airborne troops and to turn west and aid the forces protecting Caen.

Once over the Orne river, I drove north towards the coast. By this time the enemy, consisting of three British and three Canadian Infantry Divisions, had made astonishing progress and had already occupied a strip of high ground about ten kilometres from the sea. From here the excellent anti-tank gunfire of the Allies knocked out eleven of my tanks before I had barely started.... I now expected that some reinforcements would be forthcoming to help me hold my position, but nothing came. Another Allied parachute landing on both sides of the Orne, together with a sharp attack by English tanks, forced me to give up my hold on the coast. I retired to take up a line just north of Caen. By the end of that first day my division had lost almost 25 per cent of its tanks.

Edgar Feuchtinger
Quoted in Milton Shulman
Defeat in the West, 1948

Naval Operations

Innumerable duels were fought out between batteries and battleships; it was kill or be killed—silence the batteries before the batteries sank the ships. In a few moments, there were great spouts of water leaping from the surface of the sea round the battleships to show how near the defending shells were falling. It was a supreme advantage for the ships to be able to move about; this disconcerted the German gun layers while it did not discommode the Allied gunnery control. A shore battery may be unsinkable, but it stays in one spot....

The extraordinarily efficient technical training of the Allied navies made itself apparent at once. One cruiser, the U.S.S. *Quincy,* scored five direct hits in successive salvos on a heavy coastal battery, silencing it....

With the bombardment at its height, three German destroyers came dashing out of the mouth of the Seine to see what was going on—another very definite proof that the Allies had achieved tactical surprise. They caught a single glimpse of the enormous fleet and fled immediately for shelter again....

Under intense fighter protection and in the absence of any serious attempt by the Luftwaffe to interfere with them, the spotting planes were able to execute their orders in a way an artillerist dreams about. It was thanks to them that the indirect fire of the battleships, rumbling over the cliffs of the shore and the gentle slope of the back country, was guided to its mark. Some of the observers' recorded comments tell their own story:

"Got him. Finis. Next target please." And, after a "straddle," "That must be their headquarters. Generals running like billy-o."...

The strong points were knocked out

one by one, enabling the infantry to push forward…. It was the fire of the Allied ships that made this advance possible, and which enabled the gallant land forces to thrust forward and gain sufficient elbow-room for the landing. Success depended, of course, on innumerable other factors….

But the solid, indisputable fact, evinced every moment of those anxious days, was that, at sea, America and England had an overwhelming artillery which could range deeper into the peninsula than any guns the Germans could bring up in a hurry, and that, furthermore, this artillery could be relied upon to hit its target accurately, hard and often. Military circles in Berlin, during the anxious days when the world awaited from hour to hour news regarding the progress of the invasion, commented bitterly about the "red line"—the line drawn on the map marking the distance inland that the naval guns could reach. The vital part which naval bombardment played in the invasion was a surprise to the world, just as it constituted a tactical surprise for the Nazis.

C. S. Forester
"History's Biggest Gamble"
The Saturday Evening Post
12 August 1944

Utah Beach

This reminiscence of the assault was written by Bruce Bradley, a radio operator with the 29th Field Artillery Battalion.

I was attached to an infantry regiment that was to go in the first assault wave. We would be the first people to wade ashore on Utah beach…. We were told we were expendable in the first wave. I remember nobody responded to those chilling words. We were also cautioned to loosen our helmet straps as if we lost our grip on the rope ladders going down the side of the ship, we could plunge down with force enough to break our necks when the water hit the helmet rim. So I made sure I had a good grip. Better some battered knuckles than drowning.

The sea was rough and it was dark. The navy guys had remarked that they were glad they were navy at this point. I'm sure they were. We got V for Victory signs from them as they helped us over the side. Victory didn't seem possible at the time, to me. Survival, maybe.

Making the run into shore the sky was intermittently lit by explosions, some of

Soldiers wading ashore at Omaha Beach.

them of tremendous force. Bombs, shells from the battleships standing out to sea, rockets whooshing overhead, ack-ack from German positions and tracers were coming and going. An awesome display.

As we drew closer to the beach we could see the shape of the land. Also geysers of sea water were coming from shell fire, aimed at us. We had to keep our heads down. I remember I had been so tired from all the tension, lack of sleep, fear, etcetera, but all of a sudden I was not tired any more. I was very alert.

The noise of the shelling and counterfire was much louder, then there was a deafening blast and we were thrown down or knocked sideways. We had been hit by a shell. The coxswain was gone, the ramp was down, the boat was sinking. Sideways, I was thinking about how I would inflate my Mae West [life vest] somehow. I did this automatically. Most guys in that boat drowned.

My citation reads that I waded ashore, but the water was very deep and rough, so I dog-paddled toward the shore until my feet found sand. There were obstacles, triangular steel shapes, sticking up, but no barbed wire in my path. I waded onto the beach and hit the

ground. I had lost my carbine, but still had the radio. I saw what looked like a low wall ahead and I crawled for it. Gaining some cover gave me a chance to pull myself together and assess my surroundings. To my right was a dead GI about ten feet away, to my left, about thirty to forty yards away, were some GIs in the process of regrouping. As I watched they went over the wall, so I decided to flip over it also. When I looked ahead, no more sand. It was a swamp of shallow water, but I was on my way, so I started sloshing forward.

Quoted in Russell Miller
Nothing Less Than Victory, 1993

Omaha Beach

An American soldier gives his parents a vivid description of the landing.

So that all the ships would not arrive at the beach-head at the same time, we took a detour around the Channel Islands of Guernsey and Jersey, and arrived at the Omaha beach around two o'clock that afternoon. The total number of ships involved was over 6950. This fact alone was unbelievable to the

A merican soldiers being rescued in lifeboats off the coast of Normandy.

German coastal defenders. They had estimated a couple hundred ships at the most would have been available.

Our ship dropped anchor a short distance out from land because the beach-head area had not yet been cleared of mines, and roads had to be bull-dozed to get the equipment up off the beach....

On the way in to the beach, I saw one of our large ships sitting high and dry on the sand. It was an L.S.T. which was about 190 feet long. The bottom of it had been blown out by a mine. I felt very proud when I saw the American Flag, (Old Glory) blowing in the wind from the ship's mast. The Americans had landed, no doubt about it....

The beach was loaded with all sorts of equipment. Lots of oil, wrecked trucks, tanks, small boats, life jackets and bodies. Some whole, some not. I noticed a man's head that was no more than two inches thick. Another with his intestines strung out fifteen feet onto the sand.

Prior to the actual landings we were told that even though poison gas was outlawed, that if the Germans were ever going to use it, this would be the time. So when we sent in to the beach I was dressed in foul weather gear and had sprayed a poison gas repellant on all of it, including my boots. We also carried a gas mask.

We finally found a place on the beach that was clear of debris, and ran our boat up on the sand and lowered our ramp.

Joseph P. Doyon
Letter in the collection of the
Mémorial de Caen

Nobel prize–winning American novelist Ernest Miller Hemingway first made his name as a war correspondent during World War I. For the D-Day landings he was assigned as a reporter to the infantry division of the US First Army.

Out a way, rolling in the sea, was a Landing Craft Infantry [LCI], and as we came alongside of her I saw a ragged shellhole through the steel plates forward of her pilothouse where an 88-mm. German shell had punched through. Blood was dripping from the shiny edges of the hole into the sea with each roll of the LCI. Her rails and hull had been befouled by seasick men, and her dead were laid forward of her pilothouse. Our lieutenant had some conversation with another officer while we rose and fell in the surge alongside the black iron hull, and then we pulled away.

Andy went forward and talked to him, then came aft again, and we sat up on the stern and watched two destroyers coming along toward us from the eastern beaches, their guns pounding away at targets on the headlands and sloping fields behind the beaches.

"He says they don't want him to go in yet to wait," Andy said. "Let's get out of the way of this destroyer."

"How long is he going to wait?"

"He says they have no business in there now. People that should have been ahead of them haven't gone in yet. They told him to wait."

"Let's get in where we can keep track of it," I said. "Take the glasses and look at that beach, but don't tell them forward what you see."

Andy looked. He handed the glasses back to me and shook his head.

"Let's cruise along it to the right and see how it is up at that end," I said. "I'm pretty sure we can get in there when he wants to get in. You're sure they told him he shouldn't go in?"

"That's what he says."

"Talk to him again and get it straight."

Andy came back. "He says they shouldn't go in now. They're supposed to clear the mines away, so the tanks can go, and he says nothing is in there to go yet. He says they told him it is all fouled up and to stay out yet a while.".…

Slowly, laboriously, as though they were Atlas carrying the world on their shoulders, men were working up the valley on our right. They were not firing. They were just moving slowly up the valley like a tired pack train at the end of the day, going the other way from home. "The infantry has pushed up to the top of the ridge at the end of that valley," I shouted to the lieutenant.

"They don't want us yet," he said. "They told me clear they didn't want us yet."

"Let me take the glasses—or Hemingway," Andy said. Then he handed them back. "In there, there's somebody signaling with a yellow flag, and there's a boat in there in trouble, it looks like. Coxswain, take her straight in."

We moved in toward the beach at full speed, and Ed Banker looked around and said, "Mr. Anderson, the other boats are coming, too."

"Get them back!" Andy said. "Get them back!"

Banker turned around and waved the boats away. He had difficulty making them understand, but finally the wide waves they were throwing subsided and they dropped astern. "Did you get them back?" Andy asked, without looking away from the beach where we could see a half-sunken LCV(P) [Landing Craft, Vehicle, Personnel] foundered in the mined stakes.

"Yes, sir," Ed Banker said.

An LCI was headed straight toward us, pulling away from the beach after having circled to go in. As it passed, a man shouted with a megaphone, "there are wounded on that boat and she is sinking."

"Can you get in to her?" The only words we heard clearly from the megaphone as the wind snatched the voice away were "machine-gun nest."

"Did they say there was or there wasn't a machine-gun nest?" Andy said.

"I couldn't hear."

"Run alongside of her again, coxswain," he said. "Run close alongside."

"Did you say there was a machine-gun nest?" he shouted.

An officer leaned over with the megaphone. "A machine-gun nest has been firing on them. They are sinking."

"Take her straight in, coxswain," Andy said.

It was difficult to make our way through the stakes that had been sunk as obstructions, because there were contact mines fastened to them, that looked like large double pie plates fastened face to face. They looked as though they had been spiked to the pilings and then assembled. They were the ugly, neutral gray-yellow color that almost everything is in war.

We did not know what other stakes with mines were under us, but the ones that we could see we fended off by hand and worked our way to the sinking boat.

Ernest Hemingway
"A Voyage to Victory"
Collier's, 22 July 1944

Determined to follow the Normandy landings, American war correspondent Martha Gellhorn defied orders to the contrary and stowed away on a hospital ship that anchored off Omaha Beach.

June 1944
If anyone had come fresh to that ship in the night, someone unwounded, not attached to the ship, he would have been appalled. It began to look entirely Black-Hole-of-Calcutta, because it was airless and ill lit. Piles of bloody clothing had

A landing craft with medical care units takes the first casualties off Omaha Beach.

been cut off and dumped out of the way in corners; coffee cups and cigarette stubs littered the decks; plasma bottles hung from cords, and all the fearful surgical apparatus for holding broken bones made shadows on the walls. There were wounded who groaned in their sleep or called out and there was the soft steady hum of conversation among the wounded who could not sleep. That is the way it would have looked to anyone seeing it fresh—a ship carrying a load of pain, with everyone waiting for daylight, everyone hoping for the anchor to be raised, everyone longing for England. It was that but it was something else too; it was a safe ship no matter what happened to it. We were together and we counted on each other. We knew that from the British captain to the pink-cheeked little London mess boy every one of the ship's company did his job tirelessly and well. The wounded knew that the doctors and nurses and orderlies belonged to them utterly and would not fail them. And all of us knew that our own wounded were good men and

that with their amazing help, their selflessness and self-control, we would get through all right.

Martha Gellhorn
"The First Hospital Ship"
The Face of War, 1986

Gold Beach

This evocative report of activity on the British beach was written by I. G. Holley, a signaler with the Royal Hampshire Regiment.

I had already been in action in the Middle East and I felt like an old soldier, answering questions about what it is like. "Brakey," one of our reinforcements, was not yet nineteen and very apprehensive about going on his first operation. I tried to reassure him.

On our LCA there was a small keg of rum and a couple of bottles of whisky, put there by some unknown person, I never found out who, probably with the intention, good or bad, that we might need a little Dutch courage. One drink was enough for me, in the hope that it would settle a queasy stomach caused by the flat-bottomed boat tossing about in the swell. On board we had a naval sub lieutenant who, either from the magnitude of the event or from esprit de corps obtained from the rum, felt impelled to stand up and give forth a little speech on the great thing we assault troops were about to do.

Overhead there was the continuous whizz of naval shells homing in on their targets to soften them up for us. We were soon in range of mortars, a weapon we had grown to respect, and we could hear the sharp crackle of machine-gun fire. We had the word to get ready and tension was at its peak when the ramp went out. I was with the second in command of the company, a captain. He went out with me close behind. We were in the sea to the tops of our thighs, floundering ashore with other assault platoons to the left and right of us. Mortar bombs and shells were erupting in the sand and I could hear the burp-burp of Spandau light machine guns through the din. There were no shouts, only the occasional cry as men were hit and went down....

The beach was filled with half-bent running figures and we knew from experience that the safest place was to get as near to Jerry as we could. A near one blasted sand over me and my set went dead. (I discovered later that it was riddled with shrapnel). A sweet rancid smell, never forgotten, was everywhere; it was the smell of burned explosives, torn flesh and ruptured earth.

High up on the beach a flail tank was knocked out. I saw B Company's HQ group take cover behind it as a shell scored a direct hit on them. They were gone in a blast of smoke out of which came cartwheeling through the air a torn shrieking body of a stretcher bearer with the red cross on his arm clearly discernible.

We got to the sea wall, where a Spandau from a pillbox to our left flattened us until it was silenced a few minutes later. We got on the road, running as fast as our equipment would allow. A Sherman tank had collapsed in a great hole, its commander sticking his head out of the turret going mad with rage. Past this we turned off the road through a wire fence with signs on it saying "*Achtung Minen.*" A long white tape ran straight across the minefield, a corridor repeated twice again before we reached a cluster of trees where we were able to take stock of ourselves. There were six of us left.

Manuscript at the D-Day Museum
Portsmouth, England
Quoted in Russell Miller
Nothing Less Than Victory, 1993

Juno Beach

A Canadian reverend, R. Myles Hickey, accompanied the assault force on Juno Beach and later published this account.

Churchill tanks landing on one of the British beaches.

The beach was sprayed from all angles by the enemy machine guns, and now their mortars and heavy guns began hitting us. Crawling along the sand, I just reached a group of three badly wounded men when a shell landed among us, killing the others outright. That is why the report got around that I had been killed in action. Someone saw the shell hit and figured I had gotten it, too. The noise was deafening; you couldn't even hear our huge tanks that had already landed and were crunching their way through the sand; some men, unable to hear them, were run over and crushed to death. A blast shook the earth like an earthquake; it was the engineers blowing the wall.

All the while, enemy shells came screaming in, faster and faster; as we crawled along, we could hear the bullets and shrapnel cutting into the sand around us; when a shell came screaming over, you dug into the sand and held your breath, waited for the blast and the shower of stones and debris that followed; then, when it cleared a little, right next to you, perhaps someone you had been talking to half an hour before, lay dead. Others, dying, might open their eyes as you reached them. By the little disc around their necks, I knew their religion. If Catholic, I gave them Extreme Unction with one unction on the forehead; but whether Catholic or Protestant, I would tell the man he was dying and to be sorry for his sins; and often I was rewarded by the dying man opening his eyes and nodding to me knowingly. It was a hard job to get the wounded on the stretchers and carry them to the shelter of the wall. I will never forget the courage of the stretcher bearers and the first aid men that morning.

Reverend R. Myles Hickey
The Scarlet Dawn, 1980

Sword Beach

Scottish Commander Lord Lovat included this report written by a doctor in his memoirs of the war.

There was thick smoke over the beach, and the tide low but flooding. There were many bodies in the water; one was hanging round one of the tripod obstacles. The shoals were churned with bursting shells. I saw wounded men among the dead, pinned down by the weight of their equipment.

The first I came to was little Sapper Mullen, the artist. He was submerged to his chin and quite helpless. Somehow I got my scissors out and with my numb hands, which felt weak and useless, I began to cut away his rucksack and equipment. Hindmarch appeared beside me and got working on the other side. He was a bit rattled, but steadied when I spoke to him and told him what to do. As I was bending over I felt a smack across my bottom, as if someone had hit me with a big stick. It was a shell splinter, as appeared later, but it hit nothing important and I swore and went on. We dragged Mullen to the water's edge at last.

The Commando were up at the wire and clearly having trouble getting through. Hindmarch and I went back to the wounded in the water. I noticed how fast the tide was rising, and wounded men began to shout and scream as they saw they must soon drown. We worked desperately; I don't know how many we pulled clear, though it wasn't more than two or three.

"D-Day: A Second Opinion, A Medical Report of the Morning's Battle by Dr. J. H. Patterson, Royal Army Medical Corps of No. 4 Commando"
Lord Lovat
March Past, 1979

The Battle of Normandy

After the brief but glorious period of euphoria that followed the successful landing came several weeks of difficult and exhausting battle for the Allied troops. Their advance was hindered by the terrain, bad weather, and the sheer stubbornness of their enemy. Nevertheless, by mid August victory could be seen on the horizon.

General Bradley, commander of the American army troops, had to contend with not only the enemy's tenacious hold on strategic positions, but also extremely unfavorable weather conditions.

On the morning Collins jumped off for Cherbourg, we awakened to an ominous wind, a leaden sky, and a cold, scaly rain that tore at the tent flaps. Kean trudged with me to the mess tent halfway across the soggy orchard. He scowled at the weather from under his helmet. "Well, this kills Collins' chances for fighter support today."

Two miles beyond our CP, the Channel had broken into whitecaps and the surf foamed against the scarred cliffs of Pointe du Hoc. Storm warnings appeared in the weather report. But not until Wilson reported that unloading had closed down on Omaha Beach did we realize how serious was this crisis that had blown in with the storm.

On the eve of the second day of the gale, G-4 reported Omaha Beach strewn with wrecked craft as the Channel

A camouflaged German Panther tank hiding in the underbrush.

tumbled our shallow-draft vessels into junk piles on the shore. On the third day our artificial harbor on Omaha Beach buckled under the pounding of the seas. The giant concrete caissons that had been constructed in England and towed across the Channel to provide an artificial harbor for all-weather unloading were now scattered across the Omaha Beach....

When on June 22 we went down to the beach to survey the damage, I was appalled by the desolation, for it vastly exceeded that of D day. Operations on Omaha had been brought to a standstill. Even the beach engineers had crawled into their damp burrows to escape the wind and the rain. In four days this Channel storm had threatened OVERLORD with greater danger than had all the enemy's guns in 14 days ashore. Hundreds of craft had piled up on the shingle where they lay mangled beyond the reach of the surf. Where we had landed on Easy Red, a stricken rhino ferry stabbed into the side of another with each swell of the sea. The broken bow of an LCT lurched on a runnel as the seas boiled into its belly. Farther offshore another cowered helplessly as the surf foamed over the abandoned vehicles on its humped deck. A naval lieutenant in a Ranger's jacket ambled over to where we stood. I smiled wryly. "Hard to believe a storm could do all this—"

He looked carefully at my stars. "General," he said, "we would much sooner have had the whole damned Luftwaffe come down on our heads."

Omar N. Bradley
A Soldier's Story, 1951

American physician William M. McConahey wrote an account of his experiences during World War II while stationed in Germany after the war.

American troops in the *bocage.*

In my memory today, those first few hectic, flaming days of battle seem a hopelessly confused nightmare. Nothing seemed real, and days ran into nights and nights into days without meaning. Time almost stopped, and a week seemed like a month; but always in my mind I can see the never-ending stream of bleeding, dying, mangled boys whom the litter bearers brought in. In a matter of days all of us had become seasoned veterans of battle. Men rose to great heights and proved themselves men, or else went to pieces and revealed themselves as craven souls. Heroic deeds were commonplace, and usually went unnoticed.

Events seem hazy, and are not remembered clearly, but I do have painfully clear memories of watching so many of my friends come through the aid station. I hated to see the fine young infantry officers I had known so well and

American soldiers stand guard outside Cherbourg. This photograph was taken by the renowned American photo-journalist Robert Capa on 26 June 1944.

"buddied" with coming in all shot up. I remember Captain Wheeler Coy (Battalion S-3), limping in with a nasty hole in his heel from a German bullet, frowning disgustedly at having been knocked out of the fight so soon, and looking so tired and worn. I remember Major Jastre (executive officer of the second battalion), gasping for air and turning greenish from a huge sucking chest wound, while I struggled unsuccessfully to save his life....

I remember the soldier who had watched with horror and terror as a lumbering tank rolled over his legs as he lay helplessly wounded on the ground. I remember the lad whose entire lower jaw was shot away. I remember the badly wounded boy who was brought in covered with mud and grass after he had lain unnoticed in a ditch for several days.

And I remember so many others, too. Casualties were far too numerous for us to evacuate by ourselves, and many of them were hauled back to us on infantry jeeps or were carried back by comrades on makeshift litters. One bit of mute evidence of the tremendous number of wounded men treated in our station was the huge pile of discarded weapons outside. Before the injured boys came in, their weapons were dropped outside the station, and within a short time there was a large pile of Garand rifles, tommy guns, bayonets, trench knives, Browning automatic rifles, pistols, helmets, packs, blankets and so on....

To the uninitiated, it might seem strange that our division had so many casualties right away, but it is really not so surprising. We were all green, and inexperienced in war, so we did many things wrong. No matter how much soldiers maneuver and train, it takes the real thing to whip them into an efficient fighting force. Before long the 90th Division began to function like a well-oiled machine, but during those first few days all was confusion and error from top to bottom. It is always so in any division when it is first under fire. Then, too, we were facing experienced German soldiers in well-dug-in defenses in this cursed hedgerow country, ideally laid out for defense. It would have been a tough job for combat veterans, but our untried troops were given the task. And so, many men made mistakes and were killed, but those who lived learned quickly by their experience.

William M. McConahey, M.D.
Battalion Surgeon, 1966

Sydney Jary, a platoon commander in the British army, harks back to the lessons he learned in Normandy.

Normandy was a defender's paradise. It was bad tank country and our poor supporting armour lost many tanks, particularly to Panzerfausts (German bazooka detachments) firing at about thirty yards' range or less. We soon learned not to allow our "tame armour" to wander outside immediate infantry protection. In retrospect, Normandy is now a surrealistic dream, totally lacking the stark clarity of memories of subsequent battles: a pastiche of heat, dust, the stench of bloated cattle, the litter of dead tanks, rusting guns and wildly scattered grenades and small arms ammunition. We fought from one hedgerow to the next, up tortuous, overgrown sunken lanes: ideal country for the German defender but appalling for attacking infantry. However, no arm but infantry could take and hold the Normandy bocage.

It was here that I served my apprenticeship and the platoon developed its character which, despite constant depletion by casualties over the coming ten months, it would retain until the end of the war. It was also here that, imperceptibly, I became possessive with 18 Platoon. It was mine, to be guarded with an almost maternal jealousy that resented all criticism of my soldiers.

Most importantly, it was in the bocage that I began to appreciate how vital is grip: grip on oneself, grip on one's soldiers and grip on the situation. Unlike characters in novels and films, most men react nervously to real battle conditions. Discipline and regimental pride are supports but, in decisive moments of great danger, the grip of the leader on the led is paramount.

Infantry section and platoon commanders must possess the minds and hearts of their soldiers. Strength of character is not enough. Successful leadership in battle, although complex and intangible always seemed to me to depend on two factors. Firstly, soldiers must have confidence in their leaders' professional ability and, secondly, they must trust them as men. It helps, too, if a leader has the reputation of being lucky.

Field Marshal Montgomery placed great importance on the principle of "making the enemy dance to your tune." Nowhere is this more important than in the platoon and company battle. It is decisive, because if you do not dominate events your enemy will.

Sydney Jary
18 Platoon, 1987

The commander of one of the battle groups of the 21st Panzer Division, Colonel Hans von Luck, was on his way back from a three-day leave in Paris when the bombing signaling the commencement of Operation Goodwood was reported to him.

"Operation Goodwood" cost the British about 450 tanks. It was a masterpiece of preparation and logistics. And yet we were able to prevent the enemy from making a breakthrough.

Only now did we hear that on the day before "Operation Goodwood"—the start of the offensive—our own Field Marshal Erwin Rommel had been severely wounded in a fighter-bomber attack on his individual car. We could hardly take it in; to us Rommel had always seemed invulnerable.

Nevertheless, the deep defensive front set up by Rommel had held against Montgomery's attack. As late as 15 and 17 July he had checked this defense in the area of our corps. It is probably true to say that with this Rommel had denied his constant adversary the way to Paris, his last military success.

During the night of 19/20 July, torrents of rain set in, which made our relief more difficult. I shall never forget on our night march to the north the stink of the dead cows lying in the fields. On 20 July, moreover, there was a further heavy thunderstorm, which turned the battlefield into a swamp. The British air force had to stay on the ground.

Late in the evening of 20 July we learned—first through leaflets dropped

A bove: English infantrymen approaching the city retreating from their positions near Caen.

by the British, then also from our own radio station—of the attempt on Hitler's life. The older ones among us had mixed feelings; the younger were angry, "It's a stab in the back to us here at the front."…

Although the RAF launched endless attacks and the guards division, with strong patrols, tried to find a gap to the east, the days that followed seemed to us almost like a holiday. Owing to the heavy downpours of rain the flooded River Dives had become even more impassable. For me the important thing was to recreate I Battalion, which had been almost wiped out by the bombing on 18 July.…

After only a week in our defensive "resting" position the division was pulled out, to be restored to strength. We all hoped for a few days' peace to lick our wounds.

Hans von Luck
Panzer Commander: The Memoirs of Colonel Hans von Luck, 1989

A British soldier describes the triumphant reception given the liberators by the people of Normandy.

of Caen from the west. Below left: German soldiers

I entered Bayeux with the first troops. It was a scene of rejoicing as the people went wild. The streets were blocked with cheering men and women and children. The Tricolor and Union Jacks were hung in the windows. Cafes threw open their doors and pianists began to play British and French patriotic tunes. Crowds danced and shouted, "Vive Tommy," "Vive l'Amerique."

It was a scene of mingled war and peace through which I passed as I drove a jeep into the interior along part of the front line. After a dusty dreary morning, the sun burst through and the skies cleared. It was a perfect summer day. Driving through the coastal defense belt, I saw the havoc wrought by the Allied naval and air bombardment which had wrecked some roads and many hamlets which the Germans had used as headquarters....

In the fields peasants tended their sheep and cattle as if this day were no different from any other. The Allied war machine rolled past along the dusty highways, but the only sign the stolid peasants gave was a wave of the hand. It was the townspeople, like those of Bayeux, who really showed their appreciation, repeating again and again, "C'est le jour de la liberation."

Richard McMillan
Quoted in W. W. Chaplin
The Fifty-Two Days, 1944

Montgomery gives his version of how officers in SHAEF allegedly misinterpreted his strategy.

Many people thought that when Operation GOODWOOD was staged, it was the beginning of the plan to break out from the eastern flank towards Paris, and that, because I did not do so, the battle had been a failure. But let me make the point again at the risk of being wearisome. There was never at any time any intention of making the break-out from the bridgehead on the eastern flank. Misunderstandings about this simple and basic conception were responsible for much trouble between British and American personalities.

All through the fierce fighting which took place in Normandy, there was never any intention of breaking out on the eastern flank towards the Seine; reference to all the orders and instructions which I issued makes that abundantly clear. This false conception existed only at Supreme Headquarters, and none of the senior officers responsible for the conduct of the actual fighting in Normandy, Bradley included, had any doubt about the true plan. The misconception led to much controversy, and those at Supreme Headquarters who were not very fond of me took advantage of it to create trouble as the campaign developed.

Bernard L. Montgomery
The Memoirs of Field Marshal the Viscount Montgomery of Alamein, 1960

Recollections of the Inhabitants of Normandy

Many of Normandy's splendid old towns and cities, such as Caen, were ruined. Still, the exhausted and starving citizens banded together to accomplish astonishing feats of heroism. For these people yearning for freedom, no sacrifice was too great.

A Resident of Caen

Towards midnight I woke up, like everyone else, because of the dull sounds from the direction of the coast. Nobody was ever really surprised by this because we had suffered bombing raids nearly every day for several months. Meanwhile, the noise was growing hour by hour, the windows were rattling and you could see the Allied fighters by the jagged light in the sky. All along the ridge, which overlooked us, you could see blackish smoke clouds rising into the sky. The white heads of small balloons passed over the surrounding heights. The vibrations of the raid grew stronger and stronger. All over the neighbourhood, windows flew open, the shutters clattered and opinions were aired. There was no question of it: the landing had obviously occurred.

At 4 AM we all got up and bundled down to the cellar. Despite four years of waiting, nothing was ready—well, virtually nothing. Cupboards and chests were emptied in no time at all as bursting suitcases were piled up. The bathtub was filled with water as well as all available bottles. Activity was at its height.

The radio, listened to at 5:30, 6:30 and 7:30 AM, gave out not one detail. Only opinions flowed, the principal one being that "a new phase of the airborne offensive" had just started. "Please evacuate towns and villages within thirty-five kilometres of the coastline and as far as possible you will be warned of any raids."

Eventually, at 8:30 AM, the announcer stated that "the Grand Quartier general

C itizens of Normandy taking refuge in the Caen cathedral.

informs you that Allied troops have begun operations to land in the North of France." Now the North of France for us was Pas de Calais, so surely not our region. The streets of Caen were full of people, each with a bit of a smile, despite their anxiety. The noise was deafening. Electricity, water, gas, telephone—everything was cut off. Cars were driving at a most unfamiliar speed, no one showed up at work, or few did. It seemed that life as we knew it was brusquely suspended....

It was about four in the afternoon and a few folks were gathered at our entrance gate, where there was lots of talk and discussions. Our neighbour, Madame Legrain, was determined to go out and look for bread, despite the reservations of her daughter, Antoinette. As for us, we decided to go around to another neighbour, Madame Vancoppenolle. We had hardly crossed her threshold when there was a horrendous drumming of heavy motors. Madame Gournay with her son and her mother dashed for the shelter under the stairs. The earth shook and through the window by the light of an explosion we saw the aeroplanes and their bombs falling to the ground, causing an appalling impact. Mother and I joined the others at the back of the room. Monsieur Gournay and Monsieur Vancoppenolle threw themselves to the floor. The whole company trembled as they prayed. Then came a second wave of bombers, more explosions and then silence.

Those of us who had relatives in town went to look for them in a state of great anxiety, seeking news of them. Mostly they found each other but Antoinette arrived at the house and threw herself into my arms. "I've lost my mother," she cried. "I'll never see her again." I did not come to that conclusion necessarily, but

A section of Caen that was devastated by Allied bombing.

a little while later a covered handcart arrived with the body of poor Madame Legrain. There were no more coffins to be had, so M. Legrain made a coffin from wood he found around his place. The coffin was carried to the bottom of the garden and put into the ditch dug that very morning at the request of Madame Legrain.

Madame Helene Hurel
Ouest-France, June 1984
Quoted in Russell Miller
Nothing Less Than Victory
1993

Caen: The Town That Was Sacrificed

The center of the town had already been hit and fires had broken out. Then came that tragic night when tons of bombs rained down from almost a thousand bombers and the town was lit as if by daylight by flares hanging from parachutes. Many civil defense posts had been destroyed even before the rescuers could get there; many others were soon encircled by fire. In the Saint-Jean district, which was consumed by flames, rescuers performed miracles to save the wounded and survivors, particularly in the Misericord clinic.

By the second day all the firemen had been killed on active service or crushed to death in their fire station. Some rescuers worked nonstop for four days and three nights; every day and especially every night the bombing went on, interspersed with the terrifying explosion of naval shells.

Thousands of the inhabitants of Caen left the town, but hundreds of others gathered in the solid Abbaye aux Hommes or in the nearby mental hospital of Bon Sauveur. Its patients were partially evacuated and so a temporary hospital was set up where shortly two thousand wounded would be treated. In the lycée, in the old monks' refectory, the less seriously wounded were put on long marble tables. Some surgeons went on operating without a break for over thirty-eight hours. At the end of the third night one of them said: "I just can't look at any more blood."

How relentless was this file of wounded, brought in on stretchers, sometimes on wheelbarrows, on shutters, on handcarts, for there were not enough ambulances or else they could not get into the ruins any more; once even a German tank brought in a woman screaming in a difficult childbirth. At the Bon Sauveur, civilians and German or British soldiers were treated without any distinction being made; yet one day the Germans pursued a wounded civilian right into the operating theatre and killed him with a single shot.

This hospital island formed by the Bon Sauveur and the Abbaye aux Hommes, carried no special markings. Here, apart from the wounded, more that fifteen thousand refugees soon gathered. The first bombs had destroyed one of the wards, wiping out the only stock of coffins. A red cross was hastily constructed on the first day with operative fields red with the blood of the wounded until bigger red crosses could be painted on the façade of the Abbaye and the roof of the Bon Sauveur. Fearing this would not be enough, the Resistance succeeded—after many attempts—in passing information to a young woman and former prefect who warned the Allies. They had no idea that thirty-five thousand inhabitants of Caen were still clinging to their ruins. The red crosses were respected and, if a few hundred shells still fell within this perimeter, it was little in comparison to the hundreds of thousands that fell on Caen during the battle of two and a half months.

The ranks of the rescuers thinned. About a hundred died there. However, the inhabitants of Caen ignored the successive evacuation orders given by the Germans....

The situation for the civilians was precarious. Obtaining supplies of food was difficult. Fifteen thousand meals had to be served at the Abbaye aux Hommes and almost as many at the Bon Sauveur. The first-aid workers of the early days, the civil defense people, members of the

Red Cross or national organizations and other volunteers, very often students, having saved the wounded in the midst of the bombing and fought against fires for more than ten days, now went all out to ensure that food was supplied. As their stocks ran out, they cleared the communal cellars or bombed-out warehouses to bring out the supplies. Others braved the shells, sometimes between the lines, to recover abandoned or wounded cattle. However, on return how often did the Germans dispute the spoils and take their cut!...

Some wells were reopened, but the majority of the population lived in very poor hygiene conditions.

Nevertheless, the people of Caen showed admirable stoicism and selflessness. Some months later, while a cellar was being cleared out, a diary was found; it belonged to a man who died there of utter exhaustion. He had written: "I know that I am going to die and will never see the liberation for which I have waited so long, but since, by my death, others will be liberated, long live France, long live the Allies!" This expressed the general feeling at the time. Against all the odds, people were waiting for the liberation for themselves and for others.

André Heintz
"Caen During the Battle:
Account of a Witness"
Normandie 44
Edited by François Bédarida, 1987

The Americans!

Thursday 3 August
Early in the morning, M. Yver, Auguste, Emile, Roger, and I began walking to Saint-Aubin-du-Cormier, where we were going to hand over the two [German] soldiers to the police. It was raining heavily, but that did not lower our spirits.

At Saint-Aubin—where we arrived soaked—the police directed us to a school where there were already over fifty prisoners. Ours would have been quite ready to burst into grateful phrases, but we kept our distance.

When we were coming out of a café on the square a strange car, filled with four soldiers wearing khaki and large helmets covered with green camouflage net, arrived at full speed and parked under the trees. They were Americans! One of the men, a small brown-haired man with a black moustache, stood up and grabbed a telephone receiver, and then spoke into it while examining a map. Everything seemed strange to me: this nearly square vehicle, this telephone with no wires inside a car!

A curious crowd quickly gathered. We stayed silent for a second, as though struck dumb, then suddenly we all realized what the presence of these soldiers actually meant. Then we all went mad. Cries of "Long live America!" "Long live France!" "Long live de Gaulle!" rose, mixed, multiplied, soon to be drowned out by the noise of the bells. The bells rang out with great clanging and there was the enormous rumbling of an interminable column of tanks. In each tank a soldier, with a helmet on his head and earphones on his ears, was leaning out of the turret. He threw out quantities of packets of sweets and cigarettes. We did not join in the rush unleashed by this hand-out, but all the same we picked up a few packets. M. Yver, laden with Camels and Raleighs, was in heaven! He had been rationed for many days, but now he did not stop smoking.

Albert Desile
*From the Somber Years of the Occupation
to the Paths of Summer 1944,* 1983

The Longest Day

In the 1962 production of The Longest Day *(adapted from Cornelius Ryan's celebrated book), famous American, British, and French film stars play every role—from the well-known battle commanders to the anonymous soldiers.*
In 1980 the heroic exploits of the US 1st Infantry Division, "The Big Red One," were brought to the screen in a movie of the same name directed by Samuel Fuller, who in 1944 had landed on Omaha Beach with this notorious fighting team.

Stills from *The Longest Day* (above and opposite above) and *The Big Red One* (opposite below). This page: A paratrooper at Sainte-Mère-Eglise (top) and an English soldier played by Sean Connery (above). Opposite: Paratroopers descend near the cathedral of Sainte-Mère-Eglise (above) and Lee Marvin portrays a member of the American division that landed on Omaha Beach (below).

Following pages: John Wayne in a still from *The Longest Day* (p. 174) and, in a scene from the same film, Jeffrey Hunter plays an American GI (p. 175).

Chain of Command

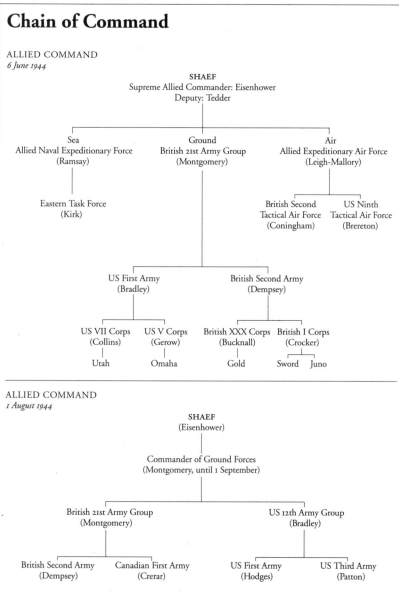

ALLIED COMMAND
6 June 1944

SHAEF
Supreme Allied Commander: Eisenhower
Deputy: Tedder

Sea
Allied Naval Expeditionary Force
(Ramsay)

Ground
British 21st Army Group
(Montgomery)

Air
Allied Expeditionary Air Force
(Leigh-Mallory)

Eastern Task Force
(Kirk)

British Second
Tactical Air Force
(Coningham)

US Ninth
Tactical Air Force
(Brereton)

US First Army
(Bradley)

British Second Army
(Dempsey)

US VII Corps
(Collins)

US V Corps
(Gerow)

British XXX Corps
(Bucknall)

British I Corps
(Crocker)

Utah

Omaha

Gold

Sword   Juno

ALLIED COMMAND
1 August 1944

SHAEF
(Eisenhower)

Commander of Ground Forces
(Montgomery, until 1 September)

British 21st Army Group
(Montgomery)

US 12th Army Group
(Bradley)

British Second Army
(Dempsey)

Canadian First Army
(Crerar)

US First Army
(Hodges)

US Third Army
(Patton)

GERMAN COMMAND
6 June 1944

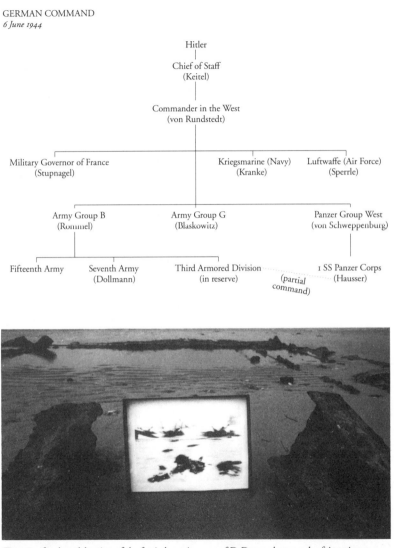

Hitler
|
Chief of Staff
(Keitel)

Commander in the West
(von Rundstedt)

Military Governor of France
(Stupnagel)

Kriegsmarine (Navy)
(Kranke)

Luftwaffe (Air Force)
(Sperrle)

Army Group B
(Rommel)

Army Group G
(Blaskowitz)

Panzer Group West
(von Schweppenburg)

Fifteenth Army

Seventh Army
(Dollmann)

Third Armored Division
(in reserve)

(partial command)

1 SS Panzer Corps
(Hausser)

In 1984, for the celebration of the fortieth anniversary of D-Day, a photograph of American soldiers landing on Omaha Beach was set in position on the shore.

Order of Battle

ALLIED

Supreme Headquarters of the Allied Expeditionary Force (SHAEF)

Supreme Commander: General Dwight D. Eisenhower (US)

Deputy Supreme Commander: Air Chief Marshal Sir Arthur W. Tedder (GB)

Chief of Staff: Lieutenant General Walter Bedell Smith (US)

Allied Naval Expeditionary Force: Admiral Sir Bertram Ramsay (GB)

British 21st Army Group

General Sir Bernard L. Montgomery (later Field Marshal)

British Second Army: Lieutenant General Sir Miles C. Dempsey
  I Corps: Lieutenant General J. T. Crocker
  VII Corps: Lieutenant General Sir Richard O'Connor (after 1 July)
  XII Corps: Lieutenant General Neil M. Ritchie (after 30 June)
  XXX Corps: Lieutenant General B. C. Bucknall (after 3 August, Brian G. Horrocks)

Canadian First Army: General Henry D. G. Crerar (after 23 July)
  II Corps (12 to 23 July): Lieutenant General G. S. Simonds

US 12th Army Group

General Omar N. Bradley (after 1 August)

US First Army: Lieutenant General Omar N. Bradley (after 1 August, General Courtney H. Hodges)
  XII Corps: Lieutenant General Gilbert R. Cook
  XV Corps: Lieutenant General Wade H. Haislip

US Third Army: General George S. Patton, Jr. (after 1 August)
  V Corps: Major General Leonard T. Gerow
  VII Corps: Major General J. Lawton Collins
  VIII Corps: Major General Troy H. Middleton
  XIX Corps: Major General Walton H. Walker

Allied Expeditionary Air Force

Air Chief Marshal Sir Trafford Leigh-Mallory

Second Tactical Force of the Royal Air Force: Air Marshal Sir Arthur Coningham

US Ninth Tactical Air Force: Lieutenant General Lewis H. Brereton and Major General Hoyt S. Vandenberg

Air Defense (GB): Air Marshal Sir Roderick M. Hill

Commander of the Royal Air Force Bombers: Air Chief Marshal Sir Arthur T. Harris

US Eighth Air Force: General James H. Doolittle

General Bernard L. Montgomery, commander of the British 21st Army Group.

GERMAN

Commander in Chief: Adolf Hitler
Chief of Staff: Field Marshal Wilhelm Keitel
Chief of Operations: Colonel General
Alfred Jodl
Commander in the West: Field Marshal Karl
Gerd von Rundstedt (until 2 July), then
Field Marshal Gunther von Kluge (until
18 August), then Field Marshal Walther
von Model

Army Group B

Field Marshal Erwin Rommel (until 17 July),
Field Marshal Gunther von Kluge
(until 18 August), then Field Marshal
Walther von Model

German Seventh Army: General Friedrich
Dollman (until 28 June), then General Paul
Hausser (until 20 August), then General
Heinrich Eberbach (until 30 August)
Panzer Group West (until 5 August),
later the 5th Panzer Army: General
Geyr von Schweppenburg (until 6 July),
then General Heinrich Eberbach
(until 9 August), then General Joseph
"Sepp" Dietrich
I SS Panzer Corps: General Paul
Hausser (until 28 July), then General
Wilhelm Bittrich
LXXXIV Corps: Lieutenant General Erich
Marcks (until 12 June), then Lieutenant
General Fahrmbacher (until 18 June), then
Lieutenant General Dietrich von Choltitz
(until 28 July), then Lieutenant General
Otto Elfeldt

Luftwaffe (Air Force)

Commander: Marshal Hugo Sperrle

Kriegsmarine (Navy)

Commander: Admiral Theodor Kranke

THE DIVISIONS

*Unless otherwise specified, the following
divisions of each army were in Normandy on
6 June 1944.*

British 21st Army Group

British Second Army:
Guards Armored Division (28 June)
7th Armored Division (8 June)
11th Armored Division (13 June)
79th Armored Division (Specialized Armor)
6th Airborne Division
3rd Infantry Division
15th Infantry Division (Scottish)
(14 June)
43rd Infantry Division (Wessex) (24 June)
49th Infantry Division (West Riding)
50th Infantry Division (Northumbrian)
51st Infantry Division (Highland)
53rd Infantry Division (Welsh) (27 June)
59th Infantry Division (Staffordshire)
(27 June)

Field Marshal Erwin Rommel, commander of
German Army Group B.

Canadian First Army:
- 4th Canadian Armored Division (31 July)
- 1st Polish Armored Division (31 July)
- 2nd Canadian Division (7 July)
- 3rd Infantry Division

US 12th Army Group

US First and Third Armies:
- 2nd Armored Division (2 July)
- 3rd Armored Division (9 July)
- 4th Armored Division (28 July)
- 5th Armored Division (2 August)
- 6th Armored Division (28 July)
- 7th Armored Division (14 August)
- 2nd French Armored Division (1 August)
- 82nd Airborne Division
- 101st Airborne Division
- 1st Infantry Division
- 2nd Infantry Division (8 June)
- 4th Infantry Division
- 5th Infantry Division (16 July)
- 8th Infantry Division (8 July)
- 9th Infantry Division (14 June)
- 28th Infantry Division (27 July)
- 29th Infantry Division (7 June)
- 30th Infantry Division (15 June)
- 35th Infantry Division (11 July)
- 79th Infantry Division (19 June)
- 80th Infantry Division (8 August)
- 83rd Infantry Division (27 June)
- 90th Infantry Division (10 June)

German Army Group B and Units of Army Group G

Seventh Army:
- 77th Infantry Division
- 91st Infantry Division
- 243rd Infantry Division
- 265th Infantry Division
- 266th Infantry Division
- 275th Infantry Division
- 343rd Infantry Division
- 352nd Infantry Division
- 353rd Infantry Division
- 709th Infantry Division

- 716th Infantry Division
- 2nd Parachute Division
- 3rd Parachute Division
- 5th Parachute Division

First Army:
- 276th Infantry Division (29 June)
- 708th Infantry Division (30 July)

Nineteenth Army:
- 271st Infantry Division (24 July)
- 272nd Infantry Division (24 July)
- 277th Infantry Division (29 June)
- 338th Infantry Division (mid August)

Fifteenth Army:
- 48th Infantry Division (mid August)
- 84th Infantry Division (30 July)
- 85th Infantry Division (5 August)
- 326th Infantry Division (30 July)
- 331st Infantry Division (30 July)
- 344th Infantry Division (mid August)
- 346th Infantry Division (29 June)
- 711th Infantry Division (29 June)
- 17th Luftwaffe Field Division (mid August)

Foreign:
- Two infantry divisions (Norway and Denmark, by early August) and one Luftwaffe division (Netherlands, by mid June)

Armored Divisions:
- 1st SS Panzer Division (late June)
- 2nd Panzer Division (12 June)
- 2nd SS Panzer Division (late June)
- 9th Panzer Division (early August)
- 9th SS Panzer (25 June)
- 10th SS Panzer (25 June)
- 12th SS Panzer (7 June)
- 17th Panzergrenadier Division (12 June)
- 21st Panzer Division
- 116th Panzer Division (20 July)
- Panzer Lehr Division (8 June)

O pposite: An American paratrooper climbs aboard his aircraft on 5 June (above), and GIs prepare to disembark from a landing craft on D-Day (below).

Chronology

1939

9 May	Alliance concluded between Germany and Italy
1 September	Germany invades Poland
3 September	Great Britain and France declare war on Germany

1940

10 May	German troops move into Belgium, Holland, and Luxembourg
June	British and French troops evacuated from Dunkirk, France
22 June	France signs armistice with Germany and Italy; beginning of the Vichy regime

1941

22 June	Germany declares war on Russia
7 December	Japan attacks US naval station at Pearl Harbor, Hawaii; America enters World War II

1942

January	Allied leaders confer in Washington, D.C.
April	Combined chiefs of staff meet in London to discuss a 1943 invasion of northwestern Europe (Operation Roundup)
19 August	Canadian troops and British Commandos attempt a raid on Dieppe, a French port on the English Channel
November	Allied forces land in North Africa (Operation Torch)

1943

January	Western Allies confer in Casablanca; Chief of Staff to Supreme Allied Commander (COSSAC) planning staff formed
May	At conference in Washington, D.C., 1 May 1944 is set as new target date for Allied invasion of northwestern Europe (now codenamed Operation Overlord)
10 July	Allied forces land in Sicily (Operation Husky)
August	American President Franklin D. Roosevelt and British Prime Minister Winston S. Churchill approve plans for Operation Overlord in Quebec, Canada
8 September	Italy surrenders to Allies
10 December	General Dwight D. Eisenhower is appointed Supreme Commander of the Allied Expeditionary Forces

1944	
1 January	Field Marshal Erwin Rommel is appointed Commander of German Army Group B
22 January	US and British troops make an amphibious landing at Anzio, Italy
15 May	Final review of Operation Overlord presented to Allied chiefs in London
6 June	Overlord is successfully launched on the beaches of Normandy
12 June	US forces capture Carentan, a town at the base of Cotentin Peninsula
13 June	British forces fail to capture Villers-Bocage; first German V-1s, flying bombs, land in southern Britain
17 June	US forces reach the southern coast of Cotentin Peninsula; Field Marshal Karl Gerd von Rundstedt and Rommel confer with Hitler at Soissons
19 June	Severe storm wrecks prefabricated harbor, or "mulberry," serving US troops at Omaha Beach
26 June	US troops capture port of Cherbourg
26–30 June	British troops launch campaign west of Caen (Operation Epsom)
2 July	Hitler replaces von Rundstedt with Field Marshal Gunther von Kluge as Commander in the West
3 July	Beginning of a US offensive to capture Saint-Lô
7–8 July	British forces clear area to the north of Caen (Operation Charnwood)
18 July	US forces capture Saint-Lô
18–20 July	British forces secure area to the east of Caen (Operation Goodwood)
20 July	Attempt to assassinate Hitler fails
23 July	Canadian First Army becomes operational
25 July	Beginning of Allied breakout from Normandy (Operation Cobra)
31 July	US troops capture Avranches; start of the move south into Brittany; British forces attack south of Caen
1 August	Command changes: US 12th Army Group is commanded by General Omar N. Bradley; new US Third Army is formed under General George S. Patton
6–8 August	Counterattack by Germans at Mortain
8 August	Canadian forces attack road between Caen and Falaise
12 August	Argentan captured by US forces
15 August	Allied forces land in southern France (Operation Dragoon)
17 August	Canadian forces enter Falaise
18 August	Field Marshal von Kluge commits suicide; Walther von Model named new Commander in the West
19 August	First units of US Third Army cross the Seine at Mantes
22 August	Falaise "pocket" is closed by US and Canadian troops; over fifty thousand German soldiers are taken prisoner
25 August	Allied troops enter Paris

Museums and Historic Sites

Principal Museums and Sites in Normandy

Arromanches
Invasion Museum (Exhibition focuses on the landing and the remains of the artificial port)

Avranches
World War II Museum

Bayeux
Battle of Normandy 1944 Memorial Museum (Detailed exhibition of the battle, complete with armor, uniforms, films, and dioramas)

Bénouville
Museum of the British Airborne Troops

Cherbourg
War and Liberation Museum, at Fort du Roule

Falaise
August 1944 Museum

Longues
Intact German coastal battery

Ouistreham
Atlantic Wall Museum
No. 4 Commando Museum

Pointe-du-Hoc
Restored artillery battery

Quinéville
Liberty Museum

Sainte-Mère-Eglise
American Airborne Troops Museum

Utah Beach
Liberty Milestone (The first of a series of milestones marking the path of the US Army from Utah Beach to Bastogne)

Military Cemeteries in Normandy

American
Colleville-Saint-Laurent (9386 graves)
Saint-James (4410 graves)

British
Banneville-Sannerville (2175 graves)
Bayeux (4868 graves)
Tilly-sur-Seulles (1224 graves)

Canadian
Bény-sur-Mer (2048 graves)
Bretteville-sur-Laize-Cintheaux (2959 graves)

Polish
Grainville-Langannerie (650 graves)

German
La Cambe (21,160 graves)
La Chapelle-en-Juger (11,169 graves)
Saint-Désir-de-Lisieux (3735 graves)

Principal Museums in the United States

Washington, D.C.
US Army Center of Military History
US Navy Museum

Principal Museums in England

London
Imperial War Museum
National Army Museum
Royal Air Force Museum

Portsmouth
D-Day Museum
Royal Navy Museum

Further Reading

Bradley, Omar N., *A Soldier's Story,* Henry Holt and Company, New York, 1951

Breuer, William B., *Mosaic of Deceit,* Greenwood, Westport, Connecticut, 1993

Bryant, Arthur, *The Turn of the Tide,* Collins, London, 1959

Cave Brown, Anthony, *Bodyguard of Lies,* Harper and Row, New York, 1975

Chaplin, W. W., *The Fifty-Two Days,* Bobbs-Merrill, Indianapolis, 1944

Crookenden, Napier, *Drop Zone Normandy,* Ian Allan, London, 1976

Dank, Milton, *D-Day,* Franklin Watts, New York, 1984

D'Este, Carlo, *Decision in Normandy,* Collins, London, 1983

Dziemanowski, M. Kamil, *War at Any Price: World War II in Europe 1939–45,* Prentice-Hall, Englewood Cliffs, New Jersey, 1987

Eisenhower, Dwight D., *Crusade in Europe,* Doubleday, New York, 1948

Funk, Arthur L., *Hidden Ally: The French Resistance, Special Operations, and the Landing in France, 1944,* Greenwood, Westport, Connecticut, 1992

Gellhorn, Martha, *The Face of War,* Virago, London, 1986

Hickey, Reverend Myles, *The Scarlet Dawn,* University of Toronto Press, Canada, 1980

Howarth, David, *D-Day, the Sixth of June, 1944,* McGraw-Hill, New York, 1959

Jary, Sydney, *18 Platoon,* Sydney Jary Ltd., Surrey, England, 1987

Jefferson, Alan, *The Guns of Merville,* John Murray, London, 1987

Keegan, John, *Six Armies in Normandy: From D-Day to the Liberation of Paris,* Viking, New York, 1982

Kemp, Anthony, *South Hampshire and the D-Day Landings,* Milestone, Horndean, England, 1984

Lamb, Richard, *Montgomery in Europe 1943–45,* Buchan and Enright, London, 1983

Liddell Hart, Sir Basil Henry, *The Other Side of the Hill,* Cassell, London, 1951

————, *The Rommel Papers,* Collins, London, 1953

Livingston, Jane, and Frances Fralin, *The Indelible Image: Photographs of War,* Abrams, New York, 1985

Lovat, Lord, *March Past,* Weidenfeld and Nicolson, London, 1978

Luck, Colonel Hans von, *Panzer Commander: The Memoirs of Colonel Hans von Luck,* Praeger, New York, 1989

Marrin, Albert, *Overlord, D-Day and the Invasion of Europe,* Atheneum, New York, 1982

Masterman, J. C., *The Double-Cross System in the War of 1939 to 1945,* Yale University Press, New Haven, Connecticut, 1972

McConahey, William M., *Battalion Surgeon,* Rochester, Minnesota, 1966

Miller, Russell, *Nothing Less Than Victory,* Michael Joseph, London, 1993

Montgomery, Bernard L., *The Memoirs of Field-Marshal the Viscount Montgomery of Alamein,* Fontana, London, 1960

Neillands, Robin, and Roderick de Normann, *D-Day, 1944: Voices for Normandy,* Weidenfeld and Nicolson, London, 1993

Norman, Albert, *Operation Overlord: Design and Reality,* Military Service Publishing Company, Harrisburg, Pennsylvania, 1952

Paine, Lauran, *D-Day,* Robert Hale, London, 1981

Ridgway, Matthew B., *Soldier,* Greenwood, Westport, Connecticut, 1974

Robertson, Terence, *Dieppe: The Shame and the Glory,* McClelland and Steward, Toronto, 1962

Ryan, Cornelius, *The Longest Day: June 6, 1944,* Simon and Schuster, New York, 1959

Seaton, Albert, *The Fall of Fortress Europe,* Holmes and Meier, New York, 1981

Shulman, Milton, *Defeat in the West,* Secker and Warburg, London, 1948

Taylor, Maxwell D., *Swords and Plowshares,* W. W. Norton and Sons, New York, 1972

Tute, Warren, with John Costello and Terry Hughes, *D-Day,* Sidgwick and Jackson, London, 1974

Wilmot, Chester, *The Struggle for Europe,* Carroll and Graf, New York, 1986

Wilt, Alan F., *The Atlantic Wall: Hitler's Defenses in the West 1941–44,* Books on Demand, Ann Arbor, Michigan, 1993

List of Illustrations

Index

English writer Anthony Kemp, born in 1939, can clearly
remember the preparations for D-Day in the Hampshire
village where he grew up. Educated at Brighton College, he
then spent several years in Germany before returning to
study modern history at Pembroke College, Oxford. After
a short period as a university lecturer, Kemp worked for
twelve years as researcher, producer, and director of award-
winning documentary programs for British television. He
has also written fifteen books on various aspects of military
and contemporary history and is a contributor to several
academic journals. Kemp currently lives in France, where
he is a writer and freelance television director.

Editor: Jennifer Stockman
Typographic Designer: Elissa Ichiyasu
Design Assistant: Miko McGinty
Text Permissions: Neil Ryder Hoos

Library of Congress Catalog Card Number: 93–73432

ISBN 0–8109–2826–4

Copyright © 1994 Gallimard

English edition copyright © 1994 Harry N. Abrams, Inc., New York,
and Thames and Hudson Ltd., London

Published in 1994 by Harry N. Abrams, Incorporated, New York

Printed and bound in Italy by Editoriale Libraria, Trieste

Acknowledgments

The author and publishers would like to thank the following individuals and institutions: Gwenn-aël Bolloré, Charles S. Dedon, Ronald Drez, Sam M. Gibbons, Sydney Jary, Lord Lovat, William M. McConahey, Madame Chalufour (Tallandier, Paris), Madame Kuhl (Bundes Archiv, Koblenz), the staff of the Imperial War Museum (London), Editions Robert Laffort, *Le Figaro*, and Angelo di Marco.

Photograph Credits

Archiv für Kunst und Geschichte, Berlin 13, 45a, 48–9b, 114, 124–5. BDIC, Paris 42–3c. Bibliothèque Nationale, Paris 24c, 24–5, 43b, 63, 72–3b, 75, 94, 108, 126, 126–7, 138–9, 150–1. Bildarchiv Preussischer Kulturbesitz, Berlin 14–5, 17a, 22b, 76–7, 80b, 111. British Film Institute, London 174, 175. Jean-Yves Brouard 21a. Bundes Archiv, Koblenz 79b, 80a, 89, 96a, 100b, 101, 162, 166. Cahiers du Cinéma 172a, 172b, 173a, 173b. D-Day Museum, Portsmouth 37a, 37b, 50–1, 72–3a, 82–3, 84–5, 86–7, 94–5a, 122–3, 124a. ECPA, Fort d'Ivry 44, 77. Imperial War Museum, London 15, 16b, 27b, 28a, 28b, 29a, 29b, 31b, 36b, 38, 38–9, 39b, 46b, 52b, 56, 57a, 57b, 70, 70–1, 76a, 90a, 90–1b, 92–3a, 103b, 104–5, 109b, 119b, 131, 133, 136a, 137b, 140, 142–3, 146, 166–7, 168, 192, back cover. Lapi-Viollet 17b, 30–1a, 102b, 112a, 122, 125c. Magnum/Robert Capa 1, 2–3, 4–5, 6–7, 8–9, 11, 48–9a, 50b, 54a, 60, 78–9a, 132, 155, 159, 164, 181b. Mémorial de Caen 16c, 40–1, 46–7a, 61ra, 61rb, 62a, 62b, 63, 64, 65, 68a, 69, 78b, 95b, 96–7, 98r, 104, 108–9a, 119a, 120a, 121c, 127, spine. Peter Newark's Pictures, Bath 14, 18, 19, 35, 39a, 74a, 74b, 80–1, 88, 90–1c, 97b, 102a, 103a, 110, 120–1, 128a, 129b, 179. Roger-Viollet 12, 22–3, 32–3, 41a, 42a, 61, 98l, 144. Royal Air Force Museum, London 92. Royal Navy Submarine Museum, Gosport 32. Tallandier, Paris 18–9, 20–1, 24a, 26, 26–7a, 30b, 34, 36–7, 43c, 45b, 52–3, 54–5, 60–1, 64–5, 91, 93b, 99b, 100–1, 106–7b, 107a, 112–3, 118b, 118–9, 121a, 129a, 130, 134, 135, 153, 156, 160, 163, 169, 177, front cover. Tank Museum, Bovington Camp, Dorset 114–5. U.S. Army, National Archives, Washington D.C. 47, 68b, 96b, 128b, 141

Text Credits

Grateful acknowledgment is made for use of material from the following works: François Bédarida, *Normandie 44*, Albin Michel, © 1987 (pp. 170–1; excerpt translated by Rosemary Stonehewer); Omar N. Bradley, *A Soldier's Story*. Reprinted by permission of the William Morris Agency, Inc., on behalf of the author © 1951 by Henry Holt and Company (pp. 132–5, 162–3); Anthony Cave Brown, *Bodyguard of Lies*, © 1975 by Anthony Cave Brown. Reprinted by permission of HarperCollins Publishers, Inc. (p. 139); W. W. Chaplin, *The Fifty-Two Days: An NBC Reporter's Story of the Battle That Faced France*. Reprinted with the permission of Macmillan College Publishing Company. Copyright © 1944 by W. W. Chaplin (p. 167); Statement to the House of Commons by the Prime Minister, Winston Churchill, *Hansard*, 6 June 1944, parliamentary copyright (pp. 146–7); Charles S. Dedon, letter in the collection of Mémorial de Caen, 1945. Used by permission of the author (pp. 140–1); Albert Desile, *Des Sombres Années de l'Occupation aux Chemins de l'Eté 1944*, Editions OCEP/La Manche Libre, Coutances, France, 1983. Used by permission of the publisher (p. 171; excerpt translated by Rosemary Stonehewer); Joseph P. Doyon, letter in the collection of the Mémorial de Caen, 1945. Used by permission of the author (pp. 141–3, 156–7); Dwight D. Eisenhower, *Crusade in Europe*. Published by Doubleday, a division of Bantam, Doubleday, Dell Publishing Group Inc. New York, 1948 (p. 144); C. S. Forester, "History's Biggest Gamble," *The Saturday Evening Post*, 12 August 1944 (pp. 154–5); Martha Gellhorn, "The First Hospital Ship," *The Face of War*, Virago, London, 1986. Reprinted by permission of Aitken, Stone & Wylie Ltd, London (pp. 158–9); Sam M. Gibbons, manuscript in the collection of the Mémorial de Caen. Used by permission of the author (pp. 150–1); Ernest Hemingway, "Voyage to Victory." Reprinted with permission of Charles Scribner's Sons, an imprint of Macmillan Publishing Company, from *By-Line: Ernest Hemingway*, edited by William White. Copyright 1944, © 1967 by Mary Hemingway. Originally appeared in *Collier's Magazine*, 22 July 1944 (pp. 157–8); R. Myles Hickey, *The Scarlet Dawn*, University of Toronto Press, Toronto, Canada, © 1980 (p. 161); Sydney Jary, *18 Platoon*, 1987. Reprinted by permission of Sydney Jary Ltd, Bristol (p. 165); John Keegan, *Six Armies in Normandy*. Copyright © 1982 by John Keegan. Used by permission of Viking Penguin, a division of Penguin Books USA, Inc. (pp. 144–5); Sir Basil Henry Liddell Hart, *The Other Side of the Hill*, Cassell, London, 1951. Reprinted by permission of David Higham Associates Ltd, London (p. 149); *The Rommel Papers*, edited by Sir Basil Henry Liddell Hart and translated by Paul Findlay, 1953. Reprinted by permission of HarperCollins Publishers Ltd, London (p. 149); Hans von Luck, *Panzer Commander: The Memoirs of Colonel Hans von Luck*, Praeger, New York, 1989 (pp. 153, 165–6); J. C. Masterman, *The Double-Cross System in the War of 1939 to 1945*, Yale University Press. Reprinted by permission of The Peters Fraser and Dunlop Group Ltd, London (pp. 136–8); William M. McConahey, M.D., *Battalion Surgeon*, Rochester, Minnesota, 1966. Used by permission of the author (pp. 163–5); Russell Miller, *Nothing Less Than Victory*, Michael Joseph, 1993. © Russell Miller 1993. Reproduced by permission of The Peters Fraser and Dunlop Group Ltd, London (pp. 143–4, 155–6, 159–60, 168–9); Bernard L. Montgomery, *The Memoirs of Field Marshal the Viscount Montgomery of Alamein*, 1960. Reprinted by permission of HarperCollins Publishers Ltd, London (pp. 135, 167); Robin Neillands and Roderick de Normann, *D-Day, 1944: Voices for Normandy*, Weidenfeld & Nicolson, London, 1993 (p. 152); Dr. J. H. Patterson, "D-Day: A Second Opinion, A Medical Report of the Morning's Battle," Lord Lovat, *March Past*, Weidenfeld & Nicolson, 1979. Reprinted by permission of Lord Lovat (p. 161); Press conference as reported in *The New York Times*, 7 June 1944, copyright © 1944 by The New York Times Company. Reprinted by permission (pp. 147–8); Milton Shulman, *Defeat in the West*, Martin Secker & Warburg, 1986. Reprinted by permission of Reed Book Services Ltd, London (pp. 153–4)